Gaelic and English

Their common origins

George McLennan

© George McLennan

First published in 2014 by Argyll Publishing

This edition by New Argyll Publishing 2018

All rights reserved. Without limiting the rights under the copyright reserved above, no part of this publication may be reproduced, stored in, or introduced into a retrieval system, or transmitted in any form or by any means (electronic, mechanical, photocopying, recording, or otherwise) without prior written permission.

For permission requests, please contact
www.newargyllpublishing.com

British Library Cataloguing-in-Publication Data.
A catalogue record for this book is available from the British Library.

ISBN 978-1-907165-39-9

Contents

Preface to the 2nd Edition — 7

Introduction — 9

Gaelic-English Correspondences — 18

    §1 b as English p or w — 19

    §2 c as English h — 23

    §3 c as English q — 29

    §4 c as English ch — 31

    §5 c as English p — 33

    §6 -chd as English ch — 36

    §7 d as English t — 37

    §8 d and st interchange — 46

    §9 f as English v or w — 48

    §10 Prosthetic F — 52

    §11 f as English s — 56

    §12 g as English y — 57

    §13 g as English c or k — 59

    §14 g as English h — 71

    §15 g as English gn — 73

    §16 Loss of initial h — 74

§17 l as English l	77
§18 ll as English ld, lt and sl	79
§19 nn as English nd and nt	80
§20 Loss of p	85
§21 s as English f	92
§22 s as English st and ks	94
§23 Moveable s	96
§24 s as English h	103
§25 s as English h in loans	105
§26 sg as English sh	107
§27 sr as English str	110
§28 t as English th	112
§29 t as English h	116
§30 Loss of English v	118
§31 a as English o	122
§32 ao as various English vowels	126
§33 ea as English i	130
§34 ea as English e	133
§35 ei as English e	136
§36 i as English e	138
§37 o as English u	141

§38 u as English o		144
§39 ua as English u		147
§40 Metathesis		150
§41 Extra vowel and schwa		154
§42 Miscellaneous		155
Index		172

PREFACE TO THE 2ND EDITION

Etymology, the study of word derivations and original roots, is a fascinating but often hazardous subject. The main problem is that scholars frequently disagree with each other and offer widely different explanations of a word's origins and connections with other languages. The famous Greek-English Lexicon of Liddell and Scott advises, in the introduction to the latest (9th) edition, that 'it was decided that etymological information should be reduced to a minimum … the speculations of etymologists are rarely free from conjecture … much rubbish'. Gaelic words have also had their share of different conjectures by various scholars, but in this book I have tried to give the most likely and most widely accepted explanations of the words listed. And, of course, most of them are fairly straightforward.

In theory, all original Gaelic/Irish words are related to other words in the Indo-European group of languages. These are, on the European side, most, but not all, of the languages of this continent (including English), and on the Indo side, Sanskrit and its modern derivatives (Hindi, Bengali etc), as well as Iranian (Persian) and related languages. Often a Gaelic word will be related to one or several of these languages but not to an English word, or at least not to one which is found in a modern English dictionary. In such cases, i.e. no extant connection to English, I have omitted these words, since the limited intention of this book is to illustrate the relationship between Gaelic and English words only.

Gaelic has borrowed many words from other languages, and continues to do so and such borrowings are, indirectly, also part of the Indo-European set-up, provided that this also applies to the language behind the borrowing. So a word such as **easbaig** 'bishop' is not a native Gaelic word, but has a good Indo-European pedigree, since it was borrowed from Latin (which borrowed it from Greek). You couldn't say this about a common borrowing such as **tombaca** 'tobacco' (see Ch. 40 under **bleoghain(n)**), which is apparently of Caribbean origin linguistically. Any words borrowed from earlier pre-Celtic British languages could also be non-Indo-European (like the case of Basque), but evidence is unlikely to be forthcoming. Quite a number of modern Gaelic words remain unexplained, certainly, but most languages have their collection of etymologically uncertain words.

There are about a thousand Gaelic words in the Gaelic-English correspondences which follow below. More could have been added, especially borrowings, but there should be enough to illustrate the connection between the languages. Mostly I've restricted examples to word roots in both languages unless other instances are not immediately obvious, in which case I've listed them. There is clearly no point, for example, in listing all the mono- compounds in English (dozens of these in most dictionaries) when one, e.g. monocle (see under **a-mhàin** §31), will do. Readers can consult their own dictionaries as required.

This new edition has given me the opportunity to review several entries and to add some new words.

INTRODUCTION

The purpose of this book is to illustrate the connection between Gaelic and English words. Since Gaelic belongs to the Indo-European family of languages, as part of the Celtic branch, it shares much vocabulary and grammar not only with the other Celtic languages (Manx, Irish, Welsh etc) but also with languages belonging to other branches such as Romance (the Latin-based languages), Germanic (English etc), Slav (Russian etc), Indic (Sanskrit etc), and so on. All this is well known to those who have an interest in such matters, but many native English speakers who have an interest in Gaelic may not be familiar with these other language families. So the following is a list of some Gaelic words and English words to which they are related, although I've occasionally mentioned another language if it makes matters clearer. Sometimes the English word may be slightly different in meaning, often with a learned reference – botanical, medical and so on – and a few are rather old-fashioned (occasionally obsolete), but the connection is usually clear enough. If the word in question occurs in a placename, as many do, I have generally mentioned this, since placenames are usually quite familiar, and sometimes retain words which are seldom used today. Some placenames cited are today relatively insignificant places – farms etc – but at one time they were settlements of local importance. If a word is not in an English dictionary, however, even though it is common in Scottish placenames, it has generally not been included; so, for instance, **feàrn** 'alder' doesn't appear despite its interesting survival in French *verne*, and the Scottish surname Fernie and English Vernon.

Adults learning Gaelic often find it quite alien, and there seems to be nothing to 'connect to' in the way that there is with French, say, or German. This is partly due to the fact that many people have picked up some French or German from school, holidays etc but have not done so with Gaelic. This may seem strange, since Gaelic is a language of this country, but ignorance of it is, or was until fairly recently, quite acceptable, even amongst otherwise well-educated people; this in spite of its impressive literary pedigree going back centuries, and the great interest in it by educated Europeans at the time of the Ossianic controversy in the late 18th century.[1] One example of this attitude can be found in English-language crossword puzzles in Scottish newspapers, where a rudimentary knowledge of French, German or Spanish is often assumed in order to help with a clue; readers are expected to know the definite and indefinite articles (*the* and *a*) and a few other common words in these languages. Such an assumption cannot be – and is not – made for Gaelic (which doesn't have an indefinite article in any case). Also, dictionaries of English – even those published in Scotland – rarely give Gaelic cognates in their etymologies, assuming, presumably, that their readers would not know Gaelic and/or would not be interested. And if any Gaelic word(s) are used in English language publications in this country, they are routinely misspelt and are often grammatically incorrect. As for house names in 'Gaelic', don't get me started....

Related words in different languages usually differ from each other in various ways because of rules or laws which affect them; once you know what the rules are, you can see the connections more clearly. A few examples from English, German and French words will illustrate this. When you see that German *Pfeffer* is English 'pepper' it suggests that initial German **pf** represents English **p**; it is then easy to see the meaning of *Pfund* (pound) and *Pfennig* (penny). Other instances are:

German initial **z** equates to English **t**, so *zehn* (ten), *zwo* (two)[2], *zwanzig* (twenty).

German **ss** equates to English **t**, so *Fuss* (foot), *Strasse* (street) *Wasser* (water).

---

[1] Though written in English, MacPherson's works claimed to be translations from Gaelic.

[2] The old feminine form often used on the telephone to avoid confusion between the normal *zwei* and *drei* (three).

INTRODUCTION

German **t**(**t**) also equates to English **d**, so *Garten* (garden), *Gott* (god), *Bett* (bed), *Wort* (word).

German **ch** equates to English **k**, so *Buch* (book), *Milch* (milk).

German **b** equates to English **v**, so *haben* (have), *sieben* (seven), *silber* (silver).

German **d** equates to English **th**, so *Danke* (thank), *Ding* (thing), *nord* (north).

German **g** equates to English **y**, so *sag* (say), *Tag* (day), *Weg* (way).

French too has its 'rules'. An initial **e** is often added to a word when the related word in English has no initial **e**. So *esprit* is English 'spirit'. Bearing this in mind, we can easily see the meaning of *esclave* (slave), *espace* (space), *estampe* (stamp), *estomac* (stomach) and so on. This feature is also found in the Celtic language family: Welsh adds an initial vowel to words borrowed from another language, as *ystryd* (street), *ystorm* (storm), *ysgol* (school) etc. The initial **y** was written as **e** in earlier Welsh. For examples of this feature in Gaelic with **f** and **s** see §10 and §23 below. It can be found in English too, with **s** (§23) and with **e**: 'scale' and 'escalate' are from the same root, and 'escape' is the basis of 'scapegoat'.[3]

Also well known is the French habit of adding **é** in place of initial **s** in other languages; so *école* is English 'school'. Fairly obvious then are *Écosse* (Scotland), *état* (state), *étudier* (study), *étrange* (strange) and so on. Another clue is provided by the French use of the circumflex to indicate an **s** previously in the word but now omitted; so *côte* is English 'coast' – *côte* will be familiar to many tourists in France, and also to many wine drinkers. So, again, obvious are

---

[3] Gaelic **sgap**, 'scatter, disperse', which may be related, also shows the unprefixed form.

château (castle), *île* (isle), *Bâle* (Basel, in Switzerland), *hôte* (host, as *table d'hôte* in restaurants) and so on.[4]

It would be surprising, then, if there were not rules regarding Gaelic and its relationship with other languages, including English. These rules reflect changes which took place in various languages as they began to move away from the parent Indo-European, perhaps around 4000 B.C. or earlier. We do not have a record of this original language but it is possible to reconstruct elements of it based on a comparison of words in languages which emerged from it. A parallel of sorts occurred within these later language groups. The Germanic family, for instance, gradually separated into at least ten different languages and even more dialects, generally mutually incomprehensible (but less so in Scandinavia); a native speaker of English, for instance, would find Norwegian quite alien, though they are both members of the Germanic language family.

Another factor is the spelling conventions of modern Gaelic, which sometimes disguise slightly the relationship of words borrowed into English. So, for instance, **s** with a slender vowel (**e** and **i**) is pronounced like an English **sh**, hence **seamrag** appears as 'shamrock' in English.

Here, then, is a collection of 'rules' regarding the differences found in related, or cognate, Gaelic and English words. Virtually all original Gaelic words, in fact, conform to these rules but I have cited for the most part only those which can be seen to relate to an English word.[5] Each rule is numbered for easy reference; and under certain words, references are frequently made to other numbers where a further 'rule' – or 'spelling rule' in the case of borrowings -

---

[4] The **s** remains in Gaelic **tastan** 'shilling', however, indicating that it was borrowed from French before the s sound disappeared. The words 'teston, testoon, tester' etc were applied to coins of various countries, those in Scotland portraying the head of Queen Mary. Modern French, after the spelling reforms of 1740, is *tête*.

[5] I have occasionally used foreign words as illustrative cognates if they appear in an English dictionary and/or are well known. This is, of course, again all part of the process of relating Gaelic to other European languages

INTRODUCTION

is discussed. So, for instance under **sgioba** in §1 there are references to §13 where Gaelic **g** relates to English **c** or **k** and §26 where Gaelic **sg** relates to English **sh**. **Sgioba** is a word borrowed into Gaelic from Norse, and a large number of words mentioned below are borrowed; the ratio is roughly 60% native Gaelic words and 40% borrowings. The English language itself has borrowed thousands of words from other languages, of course, and many of them are learned coinages from Greek and Latin, and it is to these that many Gaelic words relate, as will be seen below. This is slightly different to Gaelic's relationship with native English words, but it serves to illustrate further the interdependence of the European language families.

Some Gaelic borrowings can go back many centuries (particularly those from Latin) and sometimes are half Gaelic and half English (or Scots), as **saighdearan dearga** 'redcoats' (government soldiers during the Jacobite rebellions). And this feature continues today, as **ball-coise** 'football', **fòn-làimhe** 'mobile phone' (**làmh** means 'hand'; compare 'German' *Handy* 'mobile phone'). But this does not necessarily make them easier to recognise if you don't know Gaelic spelling conventions, which are quite different from those of English. Since Gaelic spelling is usually a reliable guide to a word's connection with English and other languages, whereas its pronunciation often isn't, this is yet another reason to ignore those who want to make Gaelic spelling easier, by which they usually mean Gaelic written in English phonetics. It's a modern instance of **mì-rùn mòr nan Gall**, since they wouldn't (you'd hope) tell a French speaker that *fils* should be spelled *feece*, or tell a German that *was* should be written *vass*.

So they need a bit of explaining. It should be added that there are often borrowings from English where good Gaelic words already exist, and such loanwords are in constant use, so **mag** 'mock' (see §13 and §31) despite existing **fanaid** and **sgeig**.

The first numbers (1-30) deal with consonants, in alphabetical order; then come vowels (31-39), followed by miscellaneous factors

GAELIC AND ENGLISH

(40-42). Vowels are present in all words, of course, so it should be pointed out here that vowels in various languages are subject to change within a word, depending on how the word is used. In English this is a common feature of verbs, indicating different tenses, and also of some nouns. Thus, 'sing, sang, sung' and the nouns 'song' and 'singsong'. All of these are just different forms of the same word-root. And with some nouns the plural has a change of vowel(s) as 'foot/feet', 'mouse/mice' etc. Gaelic doesn't do this with verbs, but it does with nouns – see below just before §31. This change of vowels within the Indo-European language families means that a cognate word in, say, English, German and Scots may have different vowels. Thus 'bread'/*Brot*/*breid* – all the same word really; likewise 'old'/*alt*/*auld*, or 'both'/*beide*/*baith*[6] and so on. In fact, with a widespread usage such as the idea of the *sea*, all five vowels appear in Indo-European cognates: Italian m_a_re (English 'marine' etc), French m_e_r, Sanskrit m_i_ras, Welsh m_ô_r, Gaelic **m_ui_r**.

Things are complicated, of course, by the eccentric spelling of English; for instance, 'build', mentioned below in §17, is pronounced as *bild*, and was written without the letter **u** in Old English. So this is something which has to be taken into account when considering the relationships of different words. Sometimes, though, it's a relief to see that there is little or no change in the vowel(s) of cognate words; thus **gàir** and the related **gairm**, meaning 'call, shout, crow', and English 'g_a_rrulous'. Another factor to note is that a Gaelic word may have more than one English cognate, and not all will show the vowel change under discussion. So **litir**, for instance, borrowed from Latin, is related to both 'letter' and 'literary'. Examples of changes of vowel from Gaelic **i** to English **e** are shown in §36; readers not too familiar with Gaelic may otherwise think that **litir** is a borrowing from English 'litter'

---

[6] **Th** in English/Scots for German **d** as mentioned above under German representations of English consonants.

INTRODUCTION

(which it isn't)[7], following other genuine borrowings like **linig** 'lining'.

The same Gaelic word may appear in more than one section, as different features of the language are illustrated, so cross-references abound. Words are in alphabetical order to make them easier to trace and are also subdivided into native words and borrowings.

Throughout the list which follows references are frequently made to voiced and unvoiced (sometimes called voiceless) consonants, since they often account for some of the changes mentioned. So it may be helpful if the difference is explained. In English some consonants, namely, **c(k)**, **f**, **p**, **s** and **t** are called unvoiced; their voiced equivalents are **g**, **v**, **b**, **z** and **d**. A voiced sound is a soft, resonant version of a consonant with vibration in your throat. An unvoiced sound is harder, less resonant and with no vibration in the throat. The voiced and unvoiced versions are close enough in sound that if you use the wrong one in the middle of a word you will still be understood. If you say 'un**t**erneath' instead of 'un**d**erneath', for instance, it won't sound quite right but it will be understood. Similarly with 'ne**k**ative' for 'ne**g**ative, 'a**v**ter' for 'a**f**ter', 'su**p**way' for 'su**b**way' and 'my**z**tery' for 'my**s**tery', to pick a few at random.

It may also be useful to explain the terms metathesis, lenition and the spelling rule, which occur frequently below. **Metathesis** is a grammatical term meaning a transposition of consonants within a word. Scots has lots of instances of this where there is a change from standard English: so *girse* and *grass*, *girn* and *grin*, *kittle* and *tickle* and so on. English itself has moved through such a process over the centuries: 'ask' was earlier <u>*acsian*</u> (old Scots *ax*), 'wasp' was *waps*, 'third' was *thridda* and so on. Consonants have simply swapped places. Since a main reason for metathesis is to make pronunciation

---

[7] Though theoretically it could be, double **t** being allowed in English but not in Gaelic. English 'lining' is, of course, from 'linen' (once commonly used for lining), and although Gaelic **lìon** is 'linen, flax' (see §42), **linig** is a gaelicised version of 'lining' (see **trèanaig** §42).

easier, it will also be found in other languages. For instance, the Spanish word for 'word', *palabra*, is cognate with English 'parable'; both are from Late Latin *parabola*, 'speech, word'. The Spanish (and Portuguese *palavra*) show metathesis from the original Latin, whereas the English doesn't. But another English word, 'palaver', borrowed from the above-mentioned *palavra*, does show metathesis.

Another factor which accounts for transposition of consonants is the treatment of consonant vowels, which are **l**, **r**, **m** and **n**. This sounds like a contradiction, but all it means is that in some languages certain consonants have a vowel-like quality. The Slav languages are well known for this, and often seem to have an unpronounceable series of consonants in a word. The Czech city of Brno, for instance, is pronounced a bit like *Berno*; but in German (it was once part of the Austro-Hungarian empire) it is *Brünn*. This illustrates an important point about consonant vowels: the **r** (in this case) can have a vowel inserted before or after it – after in the case of German – because some languages cannot cope with the combination **brn**. Again, **cn** is an acceptable start to a word (even if it is frequently pronounced **cr**) in Gaelic and some Germanic languages, but no longer in English, where it is written **kn** (e.g. 'knock') but the **k** is not now sounded. English also gets round this pronunciation difficulty by inserting a vowel, as mentioned above: 'know' and 'ken' are cognate, as are 'corn' and 'grain', and the Danish Knut became Canute in English.[8] So with Gaelic **cridhe** 'heart' the original Indo-European root would have been something like *crd* where the **r** is a consonant vowel. Gaelic put a vowel after the **r** (its usual practice), whereas other languages like Latin and Greek put it before, hence the related English 'cardiac, cordial' etc borrowed from Latin. Similarly **leamhan** with its English cognate 'elm' would have begun *lm-* in the Indo-European root.

Lenition, formerly known as aspiration, is a prominent feature of the Celtic languages. In Gaelic it takes the form of a letter **h** after

---

[8] In the placename Knoydart, **Cnòideart** 'Knut's Fiord', the mainland peninsula opposite Skye, the k sound is there in Gaelic but not in English.

INTRODUCTION

most consonants, which then changes the sound of the consonant. The new sounds are **bh** = **v**; **ch** sounded as in loch; **dh** = **gh** or **y**; **fh** becomes silent; **gh** = **gh** or **y**; **mh** = **v**; **ph** = **f**; **sh** =**h** and **th** =**h**. Grammar books and language courses will give more details. Other languages also show some of these features; note *palabra* and *palavra* mentioned above (under metathesis). Examples of Gaelic lenited consonants in Scotland's surnames and placenames are given in *A Gaelic Alphabet – a guide to the pronunciation of Gaelic letters and words* (New Argyll Publishing, 2018). Some (in addition to **f**) of the Gaelic lenited consonants may not be pronounced in a word, and this can happen in English too; contrast the sound of **g** in 'big' with its absence in 'high'.

See also 'tile' (earlier *tigele*) in §23 under **teach**.

The **spelling rule** relates to broad (**a**, **o**, **u**) and slender (**e**, **i**) vowels. The rule states that a consonant must have the same type on either side of it; if it is preceded by a broad vowel, it must be followed by a broad vowel. So Islay is **Ìle** in Gaelic, not *Ìla*. As indicated below, this rule was not applied in Old Irish, and it accounts for many modern spellings where a vowel isn't sounded but is there in conformity with the rule.

Other modern spelling conventions, such as Gaelic's restriction of double consonants to **l, n** and **r**, mean that some borrowed words may not look quite like their English equivalents. So **comann** 'society', borrowed from Latin or English, is related to 'common, community' etc but the Gaelic, in marked contrast to the English, has only one **m** but double **n** (the latter usual with a final **n** where it is part of the word root). **Comann**, (sometimes spelt **comunn**) is well known to many Scots in the form **An Comunn Gàidhealach**, 'The Highland Society', a body which promotes all things Gaelic.

GAELIC-ENGLISH CORRESPONDENCES

Each section below deals with a particular feature of the two languages. As mentioned above, the sections are in alphabetical order according to the letter or feature under discussion, beginning with consonants (§1 to §30).

§1 B AS ENGLISH P OR W

A Gaelic **b** frequently takes the place of a **p** or **pp** in a Gaelic word borrowed from another language (double **b** is not a permitted Gaelic combination). There are various reasons for this. **P** is not an original Gaelic consonant (see §20), and when found in modern Gaelic, it occurs in borrowed words – mainly from English, Norse and Latin.[9] Also, a **b** in Gaelic is pronounced like an English **p**, i.e. it is unvoiced, except when it occurs at the beginning of a word. Elsewhere in the Celtic language family, e.g. in Welsh, a **p** regularly changes to **b** in a word, one of the soft mutations. And Greek and Latin regularly interchange **b** and **p**, with the result that we have English words like 'am**b**idextrous' and 'am**p**hora', the prefix meaning *on both sides*. And this is what lies behind 'scri**b**e' and 'scri**p**t'. So Gaelic **obair** 'work' is from Latin *opus* (the stem of which is *oper-*) and relates to English 'opus, operate' etc.

Other borrowed words showing the same feature are:

abstol – a**p**ostle; borrowed from Latin, like a lot of other Gaelic ecclesiastical words.

cabar – Ca**p**ricorn, ca**p**rine. **Cabar** is 'a rafter, deer antler, caber'. Caprine relates to a horned goat. In Late Latin, from which the Gaelic is borrowed, the word was used of rafters rather like cruck timbers. English language versions of placenames with **cabar** keep the Gaelic **b**, as Cabrach 'Place of Antlers', in the south of Jura.

cabstair – ca<u>p</u>able, ca<u>p</u>ture. **Cabstair** is 'a bit', part of a bridle held in a horse's mouth. Borrowed from Latin.

caibeal – cha**p**el. Another borrowing, ultimately from Late Latin *cappella*. See also §4.

---

[9] For a few exceptions to this see §20.

caibideil – cha**p**ter. Borrowed from Latin *capitulum* 'heading'. See also §4. Another classical cognate is 'capital'.

cìobair – kee**p**er (of flocks, herds). Now 'a shepherd'. Borrowed from English.

crùbach – cri**pp**le. Borrowed from Norse. See also **crùb** §42. Related also is 'griffin/gryphon'.

cùbaid – pul**p**it. Borrowed from Latin *pulpitum* 'platform'. See also §5 and §7.

cùbair – coo**p**er. Borrowed from English.

lùb – loo**p**. **Lùb** is 'a bend, curve'. Common in placenames, as Luib in Skye, Ross & Cromarty and Perthshire, while Loch Lubnaig north of Callander, Perthshire is the boomerang-shaped loch. Probably borrowed from English.

òb – ho**p**e. Borrowed from Norse. 'Hope' is an inlet of the sea, a small bay. The word is found in Oban, 'Little Bay', and, in its more Norse form, St Margaret's Hope and Longhope in Orkney. See also §16.

pìob – pi**p**e. Borrowed from Latin.

piobar – pe**pp**er. From Latin, or possibly English.

sgioba – shi**p**. **Sgioba** is 'a boat's crew', borrowed from Norse *skip* 'ship'. Also **sgiobair** – ski**pp**er. See also §13 and §20. This is the word found in Skipness in Argyll, Loch Skipport in South Uist, and **Port Sgioba**, Gaelic for Port Charlotte in Islay.

siabann – soa**p**. Classical cognates are 'saponify' (to make into soap) and other 'sapo-' compounds. Borrowed from Latin. **Bodach an t-siabainn** 'Soap Man' was a nickname given by people in Lewis and Harris to Lord Leverhulme after he bought Lewis and part of Harris in 1918-19, hoping to develop the fishing industry.

He had made his fortune earlier from soap manufacture in England.

sùbailte – su**pp**le. Borrowed from English, and sometimes without the accent.

Although this **b** for **p** is mainly found in borrowings, instances in a native Gaelic word are:

bothar – path. **Bóthar**, an Irish word really, (hence the acute accent no longer used in Gaelic) is 'a lane, street, road'. Possibly a cattle (bò) track in origin. The etymology of 'path' is obscure, however.

carbad – carpenter. **Carbad** is 'a chariot, car' and carpenter is borrowed from Latin (which borrowed it from continental Celtic) and was used by the Romans to describe a maker of wagons, chariots, coaches etc.

sliabh – sli**p**, slo**p**e. **Sliabh** is 'a hill(side)' and is quite commonly applied to hills in the south-west, but less so elsewhere.

ubhal – a**pp**le. There was also a form *abhal*, now obsolete in Scottish Gaelic, but found in Gartnavel, **Gart nan Abhall** 'Orchard', in Glasgow; also, in its Welsh form, Avalon, the island home of dead heroes in Celtic mythology. Like the similar **Tìr nan Òg**, it was thought to be situated somewhere in the western ocean, but also had connections with Glastonbury in England because of its association with King Arthur. But Applecross, on the west coast facing Raasay, has nothing to do with apples; 'apple' there is a corruption of **abar** 'confluence, river mouth'.

There are, however, some curious instances where Gaelic reverses the above process and uses **p** instead of **b** in words borrowed from English and Norse. Common examples are **plangaid** (blanket), **ploc** (block), **pònair** (bean), **pràis** (brass), **pucaid** (bucket) and **putan** (button).

Another feature of a Gaelic **b** is its occasional use to represent an English **w** (a letter which isn't in the Gaelic alphabet). So **barantas** is from 'warranty', **bathar** from 'ware(s)' i.e. 'goods, freight'; **burmaid** from 'wormwood'; **buaic** from 'wick'; **buidhinn** from 'win' (the Gaelic **dh** is not an organic part of the word but is merely there to separate the syllables. This happens quite a lot with borrowed words). **Balt** is also used for 'welt', influenced by Latin *balteus*, English 'belt'. But Gaelic is not consistent, since in more modern borrowings you'll find **uèir** (or **uèar**), 'wire'; **watt**, 'watt'; and **vals**, 'waltz'. The last two are not Gaelic – double **t** and **v** not being a feature of Gaelic spelling, and go against the recommendation that an initial **w** in borrowed words should be represented by **u** in Gaelic.

§2 C AS ENGLISH H

A **c** at the start of a Gaelic word becomes **h** in English. So **ceud** is cognate with 'hun<u>d</u>red'. It is also cognate with 'cent, century' etc (for the missing **n** see §7), which illustrates an important feature of English: the basis of the language is Anglo-Saxon (hence 'hundred'), but there is also a large classical overlay (hence 'cent'), and many of the words listed below have both an Anglo-Saxon and a classical cognate. With the former an Indo-European **c** (or **k**) gradually (over centuries, if not millennia) changed to a **ch** sound (as in 'loch') in some languages, and from there to a simple **h** sound. This happened in English but not, for the most part,[10] in Gaelic. You can see this process in a word like Ballachulish, the village on Loch Leven. In Gaelic this is **Baile a' Chaolais** 'the Village on the Narrow Strait'. The word for strait is **caol** (English cognate 'kyle'), with a hard **c** as always in Gaelic. It has become **ch** for grammatical reasons, but the English pronunciation is *Ballahulish*, with only an **h** sound in the middle of the word. The whole process can be seen in a common surname like Docherty, which is pronounced (mostly in England) with a **k** sound in the middle, but in Scotland with a **ch** (as in *loch*) sound; but there is also a version with just the **h** sound, and the name is often written Doherty.

In some of the instances below, where the English word starts with a consonant, the **h** has now disappeared from both sight and sound, but it was there in Old English. There are echoes of this in modern Gaelic in words with an **h** sound at the beginning of a word immediately before a consonant. Thus **shnog** would be pronounced as if it were *nog* by most speakers today; the **s** is, of course, silent in this lenited form of **snog** 'nice'. It's just a matter of ease of pronunciation. In modern English there are many instances of this **c** and **h** alternation at the beginning of related words, as

---

[10] Gaelic **ch** with a slender vowel (**e** or **i**) has a lighter sound, close to an English **h** but with a bit more breathing.

'heart' and 'cardiac', 'horn' and 'unicorn', 'cornucopia' (horn of plenty) and so on.

Other Gaelic/English related words showing the same feature are:

call – halt (i.e. lame). **Call** means 'lose', and 'halt' refers to some loss of mobility. The word occurs, with metathesis, in the names Claude, Claudia and the Roman *Claudius*, all meaning 'lame'. For the Gaelic **ll** see §18.

calltainn – hazel. An earlier form of the word was **call** (supposed to be the origin of the placename Isle of Coll); the suffix **-tainn** meaning 'tree' was added later. For the Gaelic **ll** see §18. The **z** in 'hazel' is just a voiced **s** (the Old Norse form was *hasl*), which disappears here in Gaelic – see again under §18. The word appears in over a dozen placenames, Barcaldine in Benderloch, Argyll, and Invercauld in Aberdeenshire being two of the better known.

cam – ham. **Cam** means 'bent' and ham is the part of the leg above the bend of the knee. **Cam** is the root of words such as **caman,** 'shinty stick' and **camas,** 'bay' and is found in placenames, as Camusnacroise and Cambridge, but the *ham* form is also found in Hamilton and Hambledon. Probably also related are words of Latin origin meaning 'curved', as 'camber', 'camera', 'chamber'.

can – hen. Old English *hana*, 'a cock' retains the **a** vowel, as does the classical cognate 'chanticleer', a fabulous name for a cockerel (Chaucer, the Nun's Tale etc), also giving rise to the surname Chantler. **Can** means 'say', and the idea is a bird whose voice is its main characteristic.

caoin – whine. **Caoin** means '(to) weep'. In Old English the form was *hwinan*.

C AS ENGLISH H

caomh – home(ly). **Caomh** means 'kind, gentle, hospitable'. See also §32.

cas – haste. **Cas** means 'steep, rapid, sudden'. For the **t** missing from **cas** see §22.

cast – hoast. Both words mean 'a cough', the Gaelic very common, but *hoast* mainly Scots.

ceil – hell, heel, Hellier. **Ceil** means '(to) hide, cover', while the idea of hell is 'hidden below'. The Cornish surname Hellier (also Hillier, Hellyar) means a (roof) coverer, i.e. a slater or tiler. 'Heel', also spelt *hele* is mainly Scots, common in the phrase 'heel in' (of vegetables etc), 'to cover temporarily'. See also §17 and §35 for the Gaelic **i**. **Ceil** has also a classical cognate in 'con<u>ceal</u>'. See also **culaidh** below.

claon – lean, i.e. to slope. **Claon** means 'sloping, inclined'. In Old English there was an **h** before the **l** in 'lean', as there often was before consonants which now begin the word in modern English. A classical cognate is found in 're<u>cline</u>, in<u>cline</u>' etc. **Claon** is found in several placenames, e.g. Clynder in the Rosneath peninsula.

cliù – loud, <u>Lud</u>ovic. **Cliù** is 'fame', and 'loud' was earlier *hloud*; the general idea is 'much heard of, famous'. The **c** was actually present in the earlier form Chlodwig 'famous warrior'. The related Greek root was common in personal names, <u>Cleo</u>patra being probably the best known. It continues today in abbreviated forms such as Cleo.

cluas – listen. **Cluas** means 'ear'. In Old English 'listen' had an **h** at the start of the word. For the **t** missing from **cluas** see §22.

cnò – nut. The Old English form was *hnutu*. For the vowel change see §37. Classical cognates are the nuc- compounds, as 'nuciferous' (nut-bearing, of trees).

cò – who. Old English *hwa*. The **h** is pronounced in 'who', of course, as it is in other interrogatives which begin with **wh**.[11] See under **cuin** below.

coille – holt. **Coille** means 'a wood', as does 'holt', though the latter is now old-fashioned and rare. For the Gaelic **ll** see §18. **Coille** appears in many placenames, notably Killiecrankie (**Coille Chn(e)agaidh**) in Perthshire.

còrn – horn, hart. 'Hart' (i.e. stag) indicates a horned beast. Classical cognates from the same root are 'cervid, cervine' (deer-like, fawn coloured) and 'rhino<u>ceros</u>' (nose of horn). **Còrn** is an animal's (e.g. ox) horn to drink from, a widespread habit in earlier times. The word was also used in placenames to mean a sharp-pointed piece of land; in Abercorn, just west of Queensferry, it was probably the land between burns converging on the *aber*. *Aber*, the Old British equivalent of **inbhir**, a confluence, is found mainly in the east of the country. The best known example, however, is the large promontory at the south-west end of England, Cornwall, where Corn is the horn (i.e. horn-shaped promontory) and wall means Welsh or Britons, Celtic-speaking foreigners to the Saxons (hence also Wales and many other Wal- placenames, and the surnames Walsh, Wallace, Walton etc). Celtic speakers obviously wouldn't use this second element of the word, so Cornwall is **A' Chòrn** in Gaelic.

creamh – ramson. **Creamh** is 'garlic', and ramson *(*earlier *hramsa)* is wild garlic. Hramsa occurs in a number of places in England, e.g. Ramsey 'Island with Wild Garlic'.

creubh – mid<u>riff</u>. **Creubh** means 'body'; *hrif* in Old English was 'belly' (hence Modern English 'midriff'). **Bh** in Gaelic has a **v** sound.

---

[11] 'When', for example, is pronounced hwen in Scotland; in England the **h** isn't sounded in **wh** combinations, which accounts for , *inter alia*, the infamous Royal Mail postage stamp of 2007 featuring the Isle of Wight in England as the Isle of White (sic).

criathar – riddle. **Criathar** is 'a sieve' and the Old English forms were *hriddel* and *hridder*. Classical cognates, borrowed from Latin, are c<u>ri</u>bble and c<u>ri</u>bellum, the former, now obsolescent, a sieve, and the latter a spider's sieve-like spinning device. The **b** in these words corresponding to the Gaelic **th** is probably an instance of the **b/th** alternation found in the English words e<u>ryth</u>rism (borrowed from Greek, see under **fraoch** §10) and ru<u>b</u>ric (borrowed from Latin), both meaning 'red' and both from the same Indo-European root.

cridhe – heart. For the metathesis of **r** and **t/d** see §40, and for the Gaelic **d** see §7. Classical cognates are 'ca<u>rd</u>iac, co<u>rd</u>ial, ac<u>cord</u>' etc. For the last see also §42.

crò – roof. **Crò** is 'a fold, pen' (for sheep or cattle – found in several placenames, as Cromore and Crobeg in Lewis) and less often means 'a stable' or 'hut'. In Old English roof was *hrof*. The absence of the **f** in Gaelic can be explained by postulating a form *krop-* or similar as the Indo-European root. The **p** would then disappear from Gaelic as usual (see §20) and in English would become **f**. There are many instances of this last feature; compare '**p**elt' (from Latin) with its synonym '**f**ell', both meaning 'skin, hide'.

crodh – herd. **Crodh** means 'cattle'. 'Herd' was *heord* in Old English, and for the metathesis of **r** and **o** see §40.

cruach – ruck, rick. **Cruach** is 'a heap, stack' (of hay, peat etc). 'Rick' was *hreac* in Old English and the related Old Norse was *hraukr*. The word appears in the English town Penkridge, known to the Romans in Britain (4th century) as Penno<u>cruci</u>um 'chief mound'.

cruaidh – raw. **Cruaidh** means 'hard, painful', and raw was earlier *hreaw*. The general idea is 'bloody'; **crò** was an old Gaelic word (Irish really) for 'blood'. See also **cruaidh** §39.

cù – hound. The connection is seen more clearly in the plural **coin,** 'dogs', where the presence of the **n** also illustrates the classical cognate 'canine'. The **n** is part of the stem and so appears in placenames and surnames, as Caolasnacon on Loch Leven, Argyll, and Connacher. Also related are kennel, cynic and canary, the last named after the islands which had earlier been named by the Romans after a large breed of dog which lived there.

cuag – hook. **Cuag** means 'a curve'. The double **o** in hook gives more or less the same sound as the Gaelic **u**; having several different ways of writing the same vowel sound is one of the peculiarities of English, less so of Gaelic . For the **k** sound of the **g** in **cuag** see §13. More common is the adjective **cuagach** 'lame', i.e. with a leg bent in some way.

cuan – haven. Nowadays **cuan** means 'sea, ocean', but it formerly also signified 'a bay' or 'harbour', (its current meaning in Irish) as found in the placenames North and South Cuan on Seil Island, Argyll. Placenames often preserve old meanings. For the missing **v** see §30.

cuileann – holly, holm oak. For the change of vowel see §38. The word appears in several placenames, as Stronachullin, **Sròn a' Chuilinn** 'Holly Promontory', just south of Ardentinny, Cowal.

cuin – when. In Old English the word was written *hwanne*, and 'when' is pronounced today as if it were *hwen*. See also **cò**, above.

culaidh – hull. **Culaidh** is 'a garment, covering' and 'hull' is a husk, outer covering. See also **ceil** above.

A couple of borrowings are:

cainb – hemp. **Cainb** is 'cannabis', another word for hemp. Borrowed from English. Hemp, also borrowed, was earlier *hænep*.

ceall – hall. **Ceall**, 'cell', is a now obsolete[12] form of **cill** mentioned in §34. Borrowed from Latin. See also **talla** §29 for a modern adaptation of 'hall'.

---

[12] Though it has been revived as **cealla**, 'a biological cell'.

§3 C AS ENGLISH Q

Gaelic **c** is represented by English **qu**. Gaelic cannot use **q** because it is not a letter of its alphabet, and **q** is found commonly as a **k** sound (like Gaelic **c**) in other languages such as French, German etc. So a cognate of **each**, 'horse' is 'equine' etc.[13]

Other Gaelic/English related words showing this feature are:

seach(**ad**) – se<u>qu</u>ence. **Seach** and **seachad** mean 'past, beyond, alternately'. For **ea** representing English **e** see §34.

Borrowings are:

cairteal – a quarter. Both from Latin, the English via Old French.

ceist – question. Again both Gaelic and English are from Latin, the English via Old French. **Im<u>ch</u>eist** is 'anxiety, doubt', i.e. something questionable.

cidhe – quay. Borrowed from English. The **dh** is there merely to separate the vowels and isn't an organic part of the word. Gaelic does this quite a lot with modern borrowed words, especially from English.

ciudha – a queue. Again borrowed from English, with **dh** used as in the previous entry. Such words are rather artificial, especially since there are perfectly good original Gaelic equivalents, as **sreath** for 'queue', and **lamraig** for 'quay'. This is not something you could say about other words, though, such as 'quango' below.

---

[13] **Each** appears in the Gaelic forename **Eacha**(**i**)**nn**, arbitrarily anglicised as Hector.

Sometimes Gaelic uses **cu** where English has **qu** as

cuach – quaich. **Cuach** means 'cup, bowl'. Anglicised placenames usually keep the **q**, as Loch Quoich to the west of Loch Lochy. There may also be some connection with English 'quaff' (quaich had an earlier form *queff*), but the fact that the word quaich was not found in England is a difficulty.

cuid – quota. **Cuid** means 'a part, portion, share'. See also under **cuid** §5. For the Gaelic **d** see §7.

Borrowings are:

Cuaigear – Quaker. Borrowed from English. For the Gaelic **g** see §13.

cuango – quango. Borrowed from English.

cuaraidh – a quarry. Borrowed from English.

cuarantain – quarantine. Borrowed from English.

cuidhteas – quittance. Borrowed from English.

cuinnse – quince. Borrowed from English.

cuota – quota. Borrowed from English.

§4 C AS ENGLISH CH

Gaelic uses **c** at the start of a word where English has **ch**. There are plenty of instances of this alternation in the placenames of England, as, for instance, the many Casters and Chesters (see also **cailc** below). In Old English an initial **c** was pronounced **ch** with a slender vowel (e.g. *cild* = 'child'), but a Gaelic **c** is always hard (= English **k**). **K** is not a letter of the Gaelic alphabet. So Gaelic **ciste** is cognate with English 'chest'; the English is borrowed from Latin *cista*, and the Gaelic shows the influence of Scots *kist*. For the change of vowel see §36. Other instances of this feature are:

can – chant. **Can** means 'say' in modern Gaelic. Cognates with a hard **c** are 'canto, cantor, cantata' etc.

caraid – charity. **Caraid** means 'friend'. For the Gaelic **d** see §7.

curaidh – church. **Curaidh** is a 'a champion, hero'. Church (like kirk, and the name Cyril) is from a Greek word meaning 'lord, master' (now the Modern Greek for Mr and Mrs), and so a church is the Lord's (house).

An instance with **c** at the end of a word is **cròc** – crochet, crotchet, crook. **Cròc** is 'an antler'.

Borrowings include:

caibeal – chapel. Borrowed from Latin. See also §1. There is also a spelling **seipeal**, which is nearer to the English **ch** than the hard Gaelic **c**, and this is the form commonly found in placenames, as **Cnoc an t-Seipeil**, Chapelhill, Nigg, in Ross & Cromarty.

caibideil – chapter. Borrowed from Latin. See also §1.

cailc – chalk. Borrowed from Latin. For the **i** in the Gaelic see §17. The classical cognate is 'calcium' etc, and the hard **c** is also found in the placenames Calke and Kelk in the northern half of

England, reflecting Norse/Danish pronunciation from their settlement there in the Danelaw. Kelso in the Borders also shows this feature. In the south of England, however, we find the forms Chalke, Chalfont and so on. All these placenames attest to the presence of limestone.

cailis – chalice. Borrowed from Latin, as with so many ecclesiastical terms. A classical cognate is 'calix'. For the **i** in the Gaelic see §17.

càise – cheese. Another borrowing from Latin. Classical cognates are 'caseous, casein' etc. For the reasons mentioned above under **cailc**, the Norse/Danish hard **c** appears in the several instances of Keswick 'Cheese Farm'. Cheswick is also found, though its location, in the north-east of England, is surprising, unlike Chiswick in the south of England.[14] Cheesebay on the east side of North Uist, however, is thought to be a misunderstanding of a Norse word meaning *foam*. Scotland has quite a number of misspelt or mistranslated placenames, many of them well-known.

castan – chestnut. A borrowing ultimately from Latin. Also cognate is 'castanets'. The word was thought by the Greeks and Romans to be named after Castanea, a town in Magnesia, Asia Minor, presumably a famous growing area. **Castan** is the sweet Spanish chestnut, whereas another word **geanm-chnò,** based on a folk etymology (chaste nut) is the horse chestnut.

cathair – chair. The word is borrowed from Latin *cathedra* (itself borrowed from Greek) 'a chair, seat', so the Gaelic spelling shows the origin more clearly. The **t** is no longer pronounced, of course.

---

[14] There can be fluctuation, however. One of the Norfolk Keswicks was Chesewic in the 11th century.

§5 C AS ENGLISH P

Gaelic **c** at the beginning of a word is represented by English **p**. This is the well-known P & Q rule by which **c** in the Gadelic languages (Gaelic, Irish and Manx) is found as **p** in the Brythonic branch (Welsh, Breton and Cornish), and often appears as **p** in English also. So **còig,** 'five', is cognate with English 'pentagon, pentameter' etc (from Greek) as well as Latin-based 'quin' etc. See also **Caingis** below in this section.

Other instances of this feature are:

càin – pain, penalty. **Càin** is 'a tax, tribute, fine' and was originally an old Celtic legal term. The difficulty with this explanation is that the Indo-European root vowel in this case would normally appear in Gaelic as **ao**. But some modern Gaelic words with **ao** originally had **ài** instead; **gaoth** 'wind', for instance, was *gáith* in Old Irish. So **càin** may be an archaic form, something which is fairly common in legal terminology. Another possible explanation has **càin** as a borrowing from Latin *canon*, used throughout the Roman Empire to mean an annual tribute paid in kind (grain, livestock etc) and the origin of *cain* in Scots Law of similar meaning. The difficulty here is that the **a** in Latin *canon* is short, whereas in **càin** it is long, as the accent indicates. But there are other instances of this in Gaelic, as **rèilig** 'graveyard' (see §35) from Latin *reliquiae* with a short **e**.

ceann – pendragon, pennant. **Ceann** means 'head'; *pendragon* was the title of a head chief amongst the ancient Britons and Pennant, meaning 'Head of the Stream', is a Welsh placename found in pennant flag, a type of paving stone. **Ceann** appears as Kin- or Ken- in many placenames.

clann – plant. **Clann** means 'children' (origin of the word 'clan'), and plant also has this metaphorical sense of 'seed, scion', more obvious in its use as the Welsh word for 'children'.

cuid – piece. See also under **cuid**, above §3.

cuithe – pit. **Cuithe** is 'a trench', 'snowdrift' or 'cattle enclosure'. A classical cognate is 'puteal', a stone wall round a well.

An instance within the word is **iuchair** – heparin, hepatitis etc. **Iuchair** is 'fish roe' and hepa- compounds relate to the liver.

Borrowings include:

<u>cai</u>lleach – pall (-bearer), tar<u>paul</u>in. **Cailleach** means 'old woman, nun', and is borrowed (as is 'pall') from Latin *pallium*, 'a covering, cloak, pall'. A **cailleach** is thus, in origin, a veiled woman. Nunton in Benbecula is **Baile nan Cailleach**. Pall refers to the cloth covering a coffin. Pallium itself is found in English to describe an ecclesiastical garment, and the markings on birds and other creatures. **Fallainn(g)** 'a cloak' is also from Latin *pallium*, probably due to a misunderstanding of a lenited **p** (ph now has the sound f in Gaelic).[15] For the **i** in **cailleach** see §17.

Caingis – Pentecost. The Gaelic is borrowed from Latin *quinquagesima*, 'fiftieth' (day), relating to the dating of the festival.

Càisg – paschal, Pascoe. **Càisg** is 'Easter' and is borrowed from Latin. Pascoe is a Cornish surname with a reference to Easter.

clòimh – plume. **Clòimh** means 'wool', and is a borrowing from Latin, as are English 'plume' and 'plumage'. For the Gaelic **o** see §37.

còrcair – purple. Another borrowing from Latin. For the Gaelic **o** see §37. The more modern and more common form **purpaidh** is also found.

---

[15] There are other instances of this with borrowings; powder, for example, often appears as **fùdar**, and, the other way round, **praighig** for fry.

cùbaid – pulpit. The Gaelic is probably from English, itself borrowed from Latin *pulpitum*, 'stage, platform'. For the Gaelic **d** see §7.

This p/c interchange is also found within Gaelic. **Partan** 'crab' also appears as **cartan**, the latter form echoed in Scots *cart* 'crab louse', a small crab-shaped creature. Compare also the Gaelic for Cape Wrath, which is **An Carbh** in Lewis but **Am Parbh** elsewhere, and see also under **cropaig** §42.

§6 -CHD AS ENGLISH CH

Gaelic **chd** frequently represents English **ct**; in other words the Gaelic **c** is lenited and **d** is used instead of **t**, as illustrated in §7. So **ochd**, 'eight' is cognate with 'oct̲et, oct̲agon' etc. Other examples of this are:

a-nochd – noct̲urnal etc. **A-nochd** means 'tonight'.

reachd – dir̲ect̲, rect̲itude etc. **Reachd** is 'a law, a statute'. For the Gaelic vowels see §34. Also cognate is 'dir̲ge' from the use of Latin *dirige…viam meam* (direct my path) in an anthem for the dead.

uchd – pect̲oral. **Uchd** means 'breast, bosom'. The **p** is missing from the Gaelic, as normal - see §20.

Borrowings include:

achd – act. From English or Latin (the source of the English).

beannachd – benediction. Borrowed from Latin. Nowadays the word is mostly used as a rather formal 'goodbye', a bit like English 'farewell'. A 'benediction' is now **beannachadh**, and occurs in several placenames, as Bendochy, just north of Coupar Angus in Perthshire, and Bannety, near Strathmiglo in Fife.

deachd – dictate. Borrowed from Latin. For the change of vowel from **ea** to **i** see §33.

rùchd – eruct. The form **brùchd**, with the same meaning 'to belch, burst out', is also found. Borrowed from Latin. For the initial **e** in English 'eruct' see also **brù, còrd, liubhair** in §42.

Slightly different is **tiachd** – tight. **Tiachd** means 'congeal, parch'; the general idea is 'thicken'. Scots *ticht* is nearer the Gaelic. The form **teuchd** is also found.

§7 D AS ENGLISH T

Gaelic uses **d** where English has **t**. **D** is, of course, simply a voiced **t**. This interchange of consonants is quite common; as mentioned above, an English **d** is frequently a German **t**, Danish **d** is often a Norwegian **t**, and Spanish uses a non-initial **d**[16] where other Romance languages have **t**. English itself provides lots of examples, as 'ea*t*able' and 'e**d**ible' etc from the same Indo-European root. It is also a feature of Scots, as *crookit* for 'crooked' etc. In addition, Gaelic pronounces a non-initial **d** after a short vowel as **t** (so **rud** is pronounced root) and Welsh regularly changes **t** to **d** when grammar requires (the soft mutation). Also, in many of the words listed below Old Irish generally wrote **t** where Gaelic today has **d**, so it's really just a spelling convention. Modern Irish has this feature too; *punt* is pound (pre –Euro money), whereas in Gaelic it's **punnd** (though **nota**, from English 'note', is far more common, used even of pound coins). Recently, too, Gaelic has reverted from a **d** to a **t** when immediately following an **s**, so for instance **èisd** 'listen', is now written **èist**.

So Gaelic **deur** is cognate with English 'tear'(drop). Other instances of this feature with **d** at the start of a word are:

dà – two. For the change of vowel (retained in Scots *twa*) see §31. Classical cognates are 'duo, dual' etc.

damh – tame. **Damh** means 'ox', i.e. a domesticated animal. It can also mean 'stag', but this doesn't quite suit the cognate; stags have not been domesticated in this country until very recently, unlike in Scandinavia etc. It's not possible to be certain whether the various placenames with **damh**, as Ardnadam, **Àird nan Damh,** near Dunoon, and Dava, **Damhath**, a few miles north of Grantown on Spey, refer to oxen or stags; but **an Dàmhair**, October, explained as 'the rutting season', would refer to stags.

---

[16] Which, however, it often pronounces like **th** in 'then'.

darach – tree. **Darach** means 'oak', and is, in the spelling Darroch, a fairly common surname, and also appears in a few placenames, as Druimindarroch, **Druim nan Darrach** on the north shore of Loch nan Uamh, near Arisaig. A classical cognate is 'dryad', a tree nymph. Also related is **doire** 'a grove', which appears as derry in several placenames, the most well-known being (London)derry in Northern Ireland.

deich – ten. Also **deug** – teen. A classical cognate is 'decimal' etc.

deud – tooth. The vowel match is clearer in the plural 'teeth'. As mentioned above, the Old Irish form of the word ended in -t; for Gaelic **t** appearing as **th** in English see §28. Classical cognates are 'dental', dandelion etc.

do – to

do – thy, thine, thou. **Do** means 'your', the latter being the standard singular form today, unlike 'thy', which has long fallen out of use.

doras – durbar, thyroid (a door-shaped gland). **Doras** means 'door', another cognate. A durbar (door of admission) was a term well-known in India during the British Raj, and is a good example of a cognate from the Indo (more specifically, Persian) side of Indo-European. Related also is 'forest', since an Indo-European initial **dh** became **f** in Latin but **d** in English and Gaelic. Forest, borrowed from French, originally meant 'wooded countryside, the great outdoors' (as opposed to towns etc) from a Latin word for door.

draoch – trichologist. **Draoch** is 'hair standing on end' and describes someone confronted with a hair-raising situation. A trichologist is someone who investigates diseases of the hair. For the Gaelic **ao** see §32.

droigheann – trachoma, and the other trach- compounds, with the general idea of roughness. **Droigheann** is 'a thorn' and trachoma is an eye disease with scar tissue on the cornea. The word occurs in several placenames, notably Auchindrain **Achadh an Droighinn**, the centuries-old communal tenancy township a few miles south of Inveraray, now preserved as an open-air museum.

druid – thrush. **Druid** is 'a starling', though dictionaries also give 'thrush', for which the normal word now is **smeòrach**. A classical cognate (with metathesis) is 'turdine' (relating to thrushes). Loch Druidibeg in South Uist may refer to starlings.

dual – tail. **Dual** means 'a plait, ringlet of hair'. The cognate 'tail' refers to the hair of a horse's tail.

duille(ag) – thallium, thallus. **Duille(ag)** is 'a green leaf' and thallium is a recently discovered metal with a bright green line in its spectrum. Thallus is a botanical name covering lichens, algae etc.

dùn – town. **Dùn** means 'a hill fort' (defended by a stone wall), and relates to *–ton*, commonly found as a suffix, as Milton etc. The idea is a settlement enclosed by a wall, hedge etc. Dun- and Dum- are very common prefixes in placenames. Other cognates are 'down' (The Downs in England), 'dune', and 'dunce', the last a reference to the Franciscan monk Duns Scotus who was thought to have been born in Duns in the Borders. His humanist opponents objected to his pedantry and what they saw as useless learning and the modern sense of 'dunce' evolved from this.

The same feature is found with **d** inside or at the end of a Gaelic word, as:

àird – airt. **Àird** means 'direction, point of the compass'. Perhaps borrowed from English.

biodag – bite. **Biodag** is 'a dagger'. The idea is that of tearing or cutting flesh. Also probably related is bodkin, where the diminutive suffix –kin echoes the Gaelic –**ag** (a dagger being small compared to a sword).

caraid – charity. **Caraid** means 'friend'. See also §4.

casad – hoast. **Casad** means 'cough', as, of course, does hoast, though it is now heard mainly in Scotland. The word was also written **casd**, which, as mentioned at the beginning of this section is now **cast**; this recommended new spelling rather disguises its connection with **casad**. For the Gaelic initial **c** see §2.

grùdaire – groats. **Grùdaire** is 'a brewer', and groats are husked oats or other cereal – beer is normally made from barley. Related is **grùid** 'lees, sediment, dregs'.

lùdag – little. Lùdag is the 'pinkie'. Ludag is a village on a small promontory at the south end of South Uist.

madainn – matins. **Madainn** means 'morning'.

meud – mete, metre. **Meud** means 'size'. The idea is that of measurement.

nochd – nocturnal etc. **A-nochd** means 'tonight'.

sgread – scritch. A variant is 'screech', and all are onomatopoeic. For the Gaelic **g** see §13.

smachd – might (i.e. strength). See also §23.

In the following words the **d** has been lenited; such sound shifts were a feature of Gaelic in earlier centuries and are indicated today by the placing of an **h** after the consonant concerned.

bodhar – bother. **Bodhar** means 'deaf', and bother is used with this meaning in Irish English, which borrowed it from Irish Gaelic. A bothered ear is a deaf ear. The word is thought to occur in Aberbothrie near Alyth (Perthshire), though whether the reference is to a loud (i.e. deafening) stream or a quiet one (dull, deadened sound) is uncertain, the latter being more likely given its relative insignificance.

cridhe – heart. See under §2.

D AS ENGLISH T

fàidh – vatic etc. **Fàidh** is 'a prophet, seer'. For the Gaelic **f** see §9. The English cognate 'wood', now obsolete, meant 'mad, raving', a characteristic of seers.

gràdh – gratitude. **Gràdh** means 'love'.

snaidh – (Wiener) schnitzel. **Snaidh** means '(to) carve, cut' and a schnitzel is a cutlet of meat. Also **snaigh**, though the etymology is against this spelling.

suidhe – sit, seat. The classical cognates 'sedentary, sediment' etc keep the **d**. The word is common in placenames, as Bellochantuy, **Bealach an t-Suidhe** 'The Pass of the Seat' in Kintyre.

uidh – foot. **Uidh** means 'a step, journey', commonly heard in the combination **ceann-uidhe** 'destination' (i.e. journey's end). The classical cognates are 'podal, podiatry, pedal, pedestrian, pedigree,' etc all with the basic meaning 'foot'. For the **p** missing in Gaelic see §20. An Indo-European initial **p** regularly becomes **f** in English, as illustrated by paternal/father, pyre/fire, pro/for and so on. For the change of vowel see §38. See also **iasg**, §13, and **ro** §20.

D is used in many borrowed words where English has **t**, as:

bleadraich – blether. Borrowed from English.

bonaid – bonnet. Borrowed from English.

brùid – brute. Borrowed from English.

buideal – bottle. Borrowed from English.

clùd – clout. Borrowed from Scots. English 'cloth' is another cognate.

cùbaid – pulpit. See §1 above.

diathad – diet. **Diathad** is 'dinner, a meal'. Borrowed from Latin *diaeta*, as is English 'diet'. The **th** in **diathad** is there just to separate the syllables and the Latin **t** is the Gaelic **d** as usual.

fleòdradh – floating. Borrowed from Norse.

greideal – grate. **Greideal** means 'griddle', and is probably from the same Late Latin word which gave English 'grate, grid' and 'crate'.

Inid – initial. **Inid** is Shrovetide, so called because it marked the start of the lead-up to Lent. Borrowed from Latin.

ladarna – latrociny. **Ladarna** means 'bold, presumptuous', and latrocity, which appears in English dictionaries but is now really an obsolete quasi-legal term, means 'highway robbery'. Both it and the Gaelic are borrowed from the Latin word for a thief.

mòd – moot. **Mòd** nowadays refers to a Gaelic festival of music and literature, particularly the National Mod, so it is rather unfortunate that **mòd** is not a native Gaelic word, in contrast to the Welsh Eisteddfod on which the concept was based, but has been borrowed from Old English or Norse. Consequently it occurs in placenames in England, as well as Maud in Aberdeenshire. Also cognate is English 'meet'.

òraid – oration. Borrowed from Latin.

paidirean – paternal. **Paidirean** is 'a rosary, necklace'. The Gaelic is from the Latin *pater (noster)* '(our) father', the opening of the Lord's Prayer, when a rosary might be used.

pioghaid – pyet. **Pioghaid** means 'magpie', and is borrowed from Scots *pyet*. The bird is also known as 'pie', borrowed from French, which itself took it from Latin *pica*, a word familiar to ornithologists and printers. So Gaelic and Scots ignore the first part of the word, which is reasonable enough since *mag* also means 'a magpie', and is a shortened form of Margaret, used of a talkative woman. French *margot* means both 'a magpie' and 'a chatterbox, a gossip'. Scots Madge and Meg are similarly used to mean a silly, unsophisticated woman. The **gh** in **pioghaid** has no sound and has really nothing to do with the word; it is put there simply to separate the syllables.

sàbaid – sabbatical, sabbath. Borrowed from Latin.

saighead – sagitta, Sagittarius, sagacious, this last a metaphorical use in the sense of sharp (of intellect), quick on the uptake. **Saighead** means 'arrow'. Sagittarius is 'the archer', a sign of the zodiac. Borrowed from Latin. Leacnasaide, **Leac nan Saighead** 'Arrow Slab' near Gairloch, Ross & Cromarty, apparently refers to a skirmish in 1596 where a group of local Mackenzies fired arrows at an invading force of MacLeods marooned on a nearby small island.

sgàrlaid – scarlet. Borrowed from English, or perhaps Late Latin. For the Gaelic **g** see §13.

sgrùd – scrutinize. Borrowed from English. For the Gaelic **g** see §13.

sìoda – satin. **Sìoda** is 'silk', and is borrowed from Latin.

spiorad – spirit. Borrowed from Latin, originally in an ecclesiastical sense.

spaideil – expatiate. The Gaelic means 'well-dressed, natty', ultimately influenced by Italian *spaziare* with the idea of strolling about – hence *expatiate* – in one's best clothes.

sràid – stratum. **Sràid** means 'street', with which it is also cognate. A borrowing from Latin. The various early streets in England, e.g. Watling Street, are, of course, extensive roads, built by the Romans. **Calasraid** is the Gaelic for Callander in Perthshire and is thought to mean Harbour Street, for which better Gaelic would be **Sràid a' Chala**. But **Calasraid** may be an attempt to echo the English name, which itself is from earlier British/Welsh *caled* (hard) and *dobhar* (water). More straightforward is Straad on the west coast of Bute. For Gaelic initial **st** corresponding to English **str** see §27.

stad – stand. **Stad** means 'stop' and is likely borrowed from Latin; related also is 'status', i.e. standing.

staid – state. The **i** in the word (contrast **stad**, previous, which is from the same Latin root) points to Latin *statio*, 'a station, place'. When used to mean 'a country', or part of one, it is usually spelt **stàit**; the USA is **Na Stàitean Aonaichte**.

trianaid – trinity. Borrowed from Latin, though **trian**, 'a third', is an existing Gaelic word.

ùghdar – author. Borrowed from Latin.

Where English has **nt**, Gaelic usually has **d** for **t**, as before, and also drops the **n**, but often lengthens the preceding vowel by way of compensation. So **airgead** 'silver, money' has English 'argent, Argentina'[17] etc as cognates. The reverse (i.e. dropping the **d**) is a feature of Scots (*haun*/hand) but also occurs in placenames in England; Winscales was earlier Wyn**d**scales, 'Huts in a Windy Place', and Hounslow was earlier Hun**d**eslawe, 'Burial Mound of Hund (or of a Hound)'. Other instances of this feature are:

amadan – ament(ia). **Amadan** means 'idiot, fool', the idea being *mindless*, another cognate also showing **d**. Amentia is mental deficiency.

aodann – ante. **Aodann** means 'face', the idea being 'in front, before', as English 'antenatal' etc. In placenames it means 'a hill-face', and has the anglicised form *Edin*. The best known instance is probably **An t-Aodann Bàn**, Edinbane, in Skye. For the Gaelic **ao** see §32.

---

[17] Though modern Spanish has *plata* for silver, and so the country is called after the *Rio de la Plata* (River of Silver).

ceud – cent(ury) etc. **Ceud** means 'hundred'. The English word he<u>catom</u>b '(sacrifice of) a hundred oxen', a learned borrowing from Greek, also loses the **n**; Welsh *cant*, on the other hand, keeps it.

eadar – inter. **Eadar** means 'between', and is very common in placenames, as Edradour, **Eadar Dhà Dhobhar** 'between Two Waters', near Pitlochry, the site of the country's smallest distillery. For the Gaelic **ea** see §33.

<u>**onfhadh**</u> – <u>vent</u>(ilate), wind. **Onfhadh** is 'stormy and windy weather'. Another form **confhadh**, of similar meaning, occurs in Convinth, **An Confhadhach** 'Stormy Place', a few miles south of Beauly. For the Gaelic **f** see §9.

§8 D AND ST INTERCHANGE

Gaelic uses **d** where English has **st**. This is another instance of **d/t** interchange, but this time an **s** is missing in Gaelic. So **maide** 'a stick' is cognate with 'mast'. Other instances of this are:

bad – bast. **Bad** means 'a thicket, a group of trees or shrubs'. Bast is the inner bark of a tree, also called bass. Bass or basswood is a lime tree and its wood, often used to make furniture. **Bad** is found in several placenames, as Badd, Peterculter, just west of Aberdeen.

greadan – grist. **Greadan** is 'corn lightly burnt' to remove the husks. For the Gaelic **ea** see §33.

nead – nest. This has been suggested as the meaning of the placenames Nedd and Loch Nedd on the west coast of Sutherland. The word seems related to Castell Nedd (Neath) in Wales, which is on the site of the Roman fort Nidum. *Nidus* is certainly the Latin word for 'nest', but this doesn't seem likely here, and the meaning is uncertain.

sèid – hist. **Sèid** means '(to) blow' (of the wind). Hist, an exclamation to attract attention etc, is, like **sèid**, of imitative origin. For the Gaelic initial **s** corresponding to English initial **h** see §24.

In combinations of **d** and **s** in Indo-European in the reverse order from the above, i.e. **ds**, the **d** is lost in Gaelic, whereas the **s** is lost in English. Instances are:

fios – video. **Fios** is 'knowledge, information', and video-compounds refer to seeing something. Also cognate, however, are 'vision, visible' etc, which, like video, are borrowed from Latin and reflect the fact that the same Latin root could have both the **d** and the **s** forms. For the Gaelic **f** see §9.

mosach – mud. **Mosach** (also occasionally **musach**) means 'dirty, filthy' (commonly used of the weather, but also of the terrain; Mossat, about 12 miles south of Huntly, is thought to mean a muddy, damp place). But there is also the classical cognate 'mysophobia', a fear of becoming contaminated, which follows Greek, from which, like all phobia- compounds, it is borrowed. Both Gaelic and Greek retained the **s** of **ds**.

uisge – hydro. **Uisge** means 'water'. See also §13.

§9 F AS ENGLISH V OR W

Gaelic has **f** where English has **v**. An **f** is, of course, simply an unvoiced **v** in both languages, but not in Welsh, where it has the voiced **v** sound. Also, some Gaelic dialects, e.g. in Argyll, voice(d) the **f**. So **fear** 'man' is cognate with English 'virile' etc. Sometimes there is also an English cognate beginning with **w**; see under **fadhail**, **fàl**, **fann**, **fàsach** and **fios**. In the case of **fear** the **w** cognate is *wer*, found in 'wer(e)wolf' (man-wolf), 'wer(e)gild' (man-payment, i.e. blood money), and, less obviously, in 'world' (earlier *weorold*). For the Gaelic **ea** see §34. Other instances of this feature are:

facal – vocal, vocabulary etc. **Facal** means 'word'. For the change of vowel from **a** to **o** see §31.

fàidh – vatic. **Fàidh** means 'prophet, seer'. See also §7.

fàilte – valediction. **Fàilte** means 'welcome'. Although valediction refers to goodbye or leave-taking, the underlying meaning relates to good health, as 'farewell'. So 'welcome' and 'farewell' express the same sentiment, as do the Latin equivalents *salve* and *vale*, from which English 'salvation, valedictory' etc, and the surname Valentine, are derived. A further cognate is English 'weal', meaning 'prosperity, well-being'.

fàir – vernal. **Fàir** is 'the dawn', and vernal refers to springtime. The idea is that Spring is the dawn of the year after the dead night of winter.

fàisg – vex. **Fàisg** means '(to) squeeze'.

fàl – vallum. **Fàl** is 'a wall, dyke', especially one of turf. *Vallum* is borrowed from Latin but an English cognate is 'wall'. **Fàl** occurs in a few placenames, as Rhifail, **An Ruigh Fàil** 'the Slope with a Dyke' in Strath Naver, Sutherland. For the *w* of English 'wall' see also **fadhail, fàsach** and **fios** in this section.

F AS ENGLISH V OR W

falt – <u>vel</u>our, velvet. **Falt** means 'hair' (of the head), and 'velour' is a woollen fabric. Also cognate is 'wool', see §31.

fann – wane. **Fann** means 'weak'.

fàsach – vast. **Fàsach** is 'a desert, wasteland', and 'waste' is another cognate. For the **w** of 'waste' see also **fadhail, fàl** and **fios** in this section. Fasach is a village in Glendale, Skye. The root of the word is **fàs** 'empty', for which see also §22.

fastadh – vassal. **Fastadh** means 'hiring, feeing', the latter term once common in the farming fairs of the North-East. Vassal entered English at the time of the Old French feudal system, but is in origin a Celtic word, as seen today in Welsh *gwas* 'servant, lad'. Initial **gw** in Welsh equates with Gaelic **f**; so **fion** 'wine', mentioned below in this section, is Welsh *gwin*.

feachd – <u>vic</u>tor. **Feachd** means 'army', and the idea is that of a conquering host.

fearsaid – <u>vers</u>atile. **Fearsaid** is 'a spindle'. The idea is that of spinning round, turning, and the various -vert and -verse compounds also belong here.

feasgar – vesper. **Feasgar** means 'afternoon, evening'. For the English **p** see §20. Also cognate is Hesperus, the evening star; this word is borrowed from Greek' which frequently dropped the **v** sound (a Greek digamma) found in related Latin words and replaced it with an **h** sound. For another instance of this see **fion** below in this section.

feith – <u>vet</u>eran. **Feith** means '(to) wait'. The idea is that of being around for some time.

fill – in<u>vol</u>ve. **Fill** mean '(to) wrap, fold'.

fine – <u>Ven</u>us. **Fine** is 'a clan, tribe, family, kindred', and Venus is the Roman goddess of love. The general idea is that of loved ones, kith and kin.

fìor – <u>ver</u>ify, <u>ver</u>acity etc. **Fìor** means 'true'. See also §36.

fios – <u>vis</u>ion. **Fios** is 'knowledge'. Other cognates are 'wise', 'wit' and 'wizard'; for the initial **w** see also under **fadhail**, **fàl** and **fàsach** in this section.

flath – valid, Walter, Vlad(imir). **Flath** is 'a prince, ruler'. The idea is that of power and strength, which is what lies behind the personal names. The Slav names are closer to the Gaelic, whereas valid and Walter show metathesis.

With some English cognates it is easier to see only the initial **w**, which has featured a few times above, rather than **v**, as

fèith – withe. **Fèith** is 'a sinew, vein'. The idea is that of a flexible cord, fibre.

feun – wain. Also cognate is 'wagon' (Old English *waegn*); for the disappearance of the **g** in Gaelic before **n** see §15.

fianais – witness. Earlier Irish had a **d** before the **n**, and its disappearance is quite normal in Gaelic.

fiodh – wood. **Fiodh** is 'a piece of wood, timber'; a wood (i.e. forest) is **coille**, mentioned in §2. The two senses rather overlap in placenames such as Glen Fiddich, **Gleann Fhiodhaich**.

foill – wile. **Foill** means 'treachery, deceit'.

There are also borrowings:

fadhail – <u>vade</u> mecum. **Fadhail** – also **faodhail** – is 'a ford' (inter-island). Borrowed from Norse. *Vade mecum* is a small handbook (literally 'go with me') which can be carried in a pocket, and the underlying meaning of **fadhail** is a place in water where you can go on foot when the tide is out. A non-classical cognate is English 'wade'; for the initial **w** see also **fàl**, **fàsach** and **fios** below. Benbecula is a garbled version of **Beinn nam Fadhla** 'the hill of the fords'; the island (a hill only in relation to the sea around) lies between North and South Uist and could be reached from both on foot at low tide. It is now, of course, linked by causeways to North and South Uist.

fànas – vain. **Fànas** means '(outer) space'. The idea is 'emptiness', which is the meaning of the Latin word from which the Gaelic is borrowed.

feart – virtue. **Feart** means 'an attribute, quality'. Borrowed from Latin. For the Gaelic **ea** becoming **i** in English see §33.

fèileadh – veil, ve̲lum, reve̲al. **Fèileadh** means 'kilt' (sometimes with **beag,** 'small', added); filibeg (various spellings) is an old-fashioned rendering of this. The idea is 'a covering'. Borrowed from Latin.

fion – vine. From Latin *vinum*. **Fìon** is 'wine', and the Gaelic form suggests that it was borrowed when the Latin **v** had roughly the sound it has in English (e.g. **v**an); this was happening during the early centuries A.D. Before this change **v** had a **w** sound (as in English **w**et), and English '**w**ine', another cognate, shows the influence of this. Also cognate is o̲e̲n̲o̲phile 'a wine lover' and other oeno- compounds; for the missing f/v see under **feasgar** above in this section. **Fìon** was applied to several streams, wells, etc, because of their medicinal qualities; Loch Fyne in Argyll is probably the best known.

§10 PROSTHETIC F

Sometimes **f** has been added to the beginning of a word though it has no connection with that word. The same thing happens with **s**, see §24. In the case of **f**, it is thought that the fact that a lenited **f** has no sound is what lies behind this; in other words **f**, in common with other consonants, sometimes has an **h** after it for reasons of grammar, and the resulting **fh** is silent. So by writing, say, **fàinne** instead of the correct form **àinne**, 'a ring', you can see that it hasn't been lenited; had it been **àinne**, it wouldn't be clear in speech whether this was **fhàinne** or **àinne**, since both sound the same. Whatever the reasons, and there is no doubt that grammatical misunderstandings have sometimes been responsible, the following, because of related English words, show that the **f** doesn't belong in the Gaelic word:[18]

fàinne – annular, anus. **Fàinne** 'a ring', as mentioned above, is the normal form today, though it is strictly incorrect.

fàs – wax. **Fàs** means 'grow, increase'. Only the form with **f** is found. See also §22.

fliuch – liquid. **Fliuch** means 'wet'. **Fliche** 'moisture' is closer to the English vowel sound. Related, with metathesis, is **failc** 'to water, wash'.

Borrowings are:

failm – helm. Borrowed from Norse.

---

[18] One could compare the use in England of **r** to avoid hiatus – *drawring* for *drawing*, etc. The second **r** is not a part of the word. Because such speakers don't sound final **r** unless the next word begins with a vowel, 'hear' is pronounced *hea*, but 'hear of' retains the **r** sound to avoid any hiatus. By analogy 'idea of' is pronounced *idear of*, creating a new "word" *idear*. Many readers may recall the English sergeant major in Sir Compton MacKenzie's *Whisky Galore* reminiscing about 'poor chaps in Africar and Burmar and Indiar and …'

PROSTHETIC F

falc – auk. Borrowed from Norse, as is the English. Only the form with **f** is found in Gaelic, though it doesn't appear in the Norse.

Sometimes the opposite occurs and the **f** has been dropped, though it should be there, as:

raineach – fern. You can see the relationship between fern and **raineach** when you add the **f** and take account of the metathesis (the **r** changing places with the vowel). The correct form with **f** is found in Islay as **froineach**, 'fern, bracken', **fraineach** in Sutherland, but the standard form is of long standing, to judge by its appearance in placenames, Rannoch in Perthshire being the best known. But another theory is that the Indo-European root began with a **p**, which disappeared from Gaelic, as normal, and became **f** in English (see §20).

ugan – suffocate, fauces. **Ugan** is 'the front of the neck, upper breast area', and fauces is a medical term for the throat. For the Gaelic **g** see §13.

Borrowings are:

easag – pheasant (earlier *fesant*). Borrowed from English, which took it from Anglo-French. Pheasants are thought to have been introduced to Britain by the Romans and the word is of Latin origin (from an area near the Black Sea). The Germanic and Celtic languages do not have a native word for pheasant, but use *fesant* or similar, or else a circumlocution (cock of the woods etc).

eileatrom – feretory, feral. **Eileatrom** is 'a hearse, bier'. A feretory is a portable shrine, a litter for carrying sacred relics in the Roman Catholic Church, and feral means 'funereal'. For the **l/r** interchange see under **sroghall** §21. Borrowed from Latin (which borrowed it from Greek). For the connection between feretory and **beir** see **beir** §35.

iarmailt – firmament. Borrowed from Latin.

Sometimes a word is found both with and without the initial **f**. An arrow maker is both **leistear** and **fleistear**. The latter is the correct form, as it has been borrowed from Scots but ultimately from French – *flèche* being 'arrow' in modern French. The origin of *flèche* is uncertain, but if it has been borrowed from the earlier Celtic equivalent of Gaelic **fleasg** 'rod, wand', as is sometimes thought, then this reinforces the position of the initial **f**.

There are also instances where the **f** is missing in the English cognate:

fraoch – erica. Both words mean 'heather, heath', and the English word erica (Latin really, which borrowed it from Greek) has an **e** added on the front, something which Greek occasionally did with a word beginning with **r**. Another instance of this with a Gaelic connection is **ruadh,** 'red', which has the cognate 'erythrism' (redness), and other erythro- compounds derived from Greek.[19] For the vowel change see §32. Not surprisingly, **fraoch** appears in several placenames, as Freuchie in Fife, and Lewis is also known as **Eilean Fraoich** or **Eilean an Fhraoich** 'Heather Island'.

fras – rosemary, roscid. **Fras** means 'a shower' (of rain etc) and rosemary (earlier *rosmarine*) is 'sea dew' – it is often found growing by the sea. Roscid is a classical cognate meaning 'dewy', but the Latin *ros*, from which roscid comes, is also used of various falling liquids, such as rain. For the vowel change see §31.

freumh – ramus, ramify etc. **Freumh** means 'a root', whereas *ramus* is 'a branch', an extension of the root. Related is the surname Ramage.

There are instances of this within Gaelic itself. **Eige** 'a web' is thought to relate to **fighe** 'weaving', with the former losing the **f** sound from the Indo-European root. Both forms can occur in

---

[19] The Greek vowel **u** is generally transliterated **y** in English derivatives; for the Gaelic **d** but English **t** see §7.

modern Gaelic dialects, as **eagal** and **feagal** 'fear'. And visitors to Ireland will be familiar with *oscailte* 'open', which is **fosgailte** in this country (and in Donegal).

Here perhaps may belong **foinne** – wen. **Foinne** is 'a wart' and a wen is a cyst on the body. **W** is not a letter of the Gaelic alphabet and is usually represented by the vowel **u** in Gaelic borrowings. It is possible, however, that the Gaelic may reflect an earlier Germanic sound of **w** as a **v**, in which case there may be an echo of English **v** where Gaelic has **f**, as mentioned in §9.

§11 F AS ENGLISH S

An initial **s** in English sometimes appears as **f** in Gaelic, though not very common. A couple of instances are:

fonn – sound. **Fonn** is 'a tune'. For the Gaelic **nn** in place of English **nd** see §19.

follaiseach – selenic. **Follaiseach** means 'clear, brought to light', and selenic means 'of the moon'. **Solas** 'a light' is also related, as are the female forenames Helen and, probably, Selina (moon, bright).

§12 G AS ENGLISH Y

A Gaelic **g** often appears where English has **y**, usually, but not always (see **balg** below), at the beginning of a word. This is also a common interchange between English and German, as mentioned in the introductory remarks. It also appears in English placenames, hence the common Burgh contrasted with Bury, both being versions of the same word, meaning, in this case, 'town'. The connection is clearer in Gaelic because a lenited **g** (i.e. **gh**) is pronounced like a **y** (English **y**es) when next to an **e** or **i**. So a word borrowed from English, as 'yacht', is written **gheat** in Gaelic, giving roughly the same sound as the English. In Modern Greek a **g** (gamma) is pronounced **y** in similar circumstances, and in Old English words now beginning with **y** began with **g**; 'yearn', for example, was earlier *giernan*. This feature is still found in Scots; *yett*, for instance, is English 'gate'. Gaelic instances are:

balg – belly, bellows. **Balg** is 'a bag, an inflatable bladder'. See also §42. Also **balgam** 'a mouthful' (of liquid). Balgom Street in Campbeltown is supposed to have been the site of several inns.

gad – yard. **Gad** is 'a rod, twig, withe', and this was the earlier meaning of 'yard'; only later did it acquire the specific meaning of three feet.

geal – yellow. **Geal** is 'white, bright'. **A' ghealach**, for instance, is 'the moon'. Words for colours often correspond rather vaguely in different languages.

go(i)rt – yearn. **Go(i)rt** is 'famine'.

minig – many. **Minig** means 'often'. 'Many' was *manig* in Old English.

A couple of borrowings are:

gàrradh – yard. **Gàrradh** means 'garden'. Borrowed from Norse, it occurs in a few placenames, as Garrabost in Lewis.

geòla – yawl. Borrowed from Norse.

§13 G AS ENGLISH C OR K

A **g** in Gaelic takes the place of English **c** or **k**. This is not really surprising since **g** is a voiced **c** (or **k**) and is pronounced in Gaelic like English **c** or **k** unless it's the first letter of a word, or preceded by **n**. In Old Irish **c** was written in instead of **g** in many such instances, and Welsh shows a similar tendency, as *bach* for Gaelic **beag**, 'small'. Also, in the Roman alphabet (the basis of most European-language alphabets, including English and Gaelic) **c** originally had the sound of **g**, representing the Greek gamma (**g**); both are the third letter in their respective alphabets. **G** was a later addition to the Roman alphabet. English itself has examples of this interchange, as '**k**nee' and its classical cognate '**g**enuflect'. (The **k** in 'knee' and similar words was sounded in Scots until fairly recently.) And the **g** is retained in the Gaelic cognate **glùn**. So Gaelic **gin,** 'beget, generate, produce', is related to English 'kin, kind' and classical cognates 'genus, generate' etc, and is also the source of **nighean** (earlier *ingen*) 'daughter'. Other instances with initial **g** (always sounded hard, as in English 'got') are:

galar – cholera. **Galar** means 'disease'. Another cognate is 'gall'. In view of Welsh *galar* meaning 'mourning, sorrow', however, the Gaelic may have some connection with **gal** 'weep'.

gean – kind(ly). **Gean** means 'good humour, pleasant mood'.

gearan – care. **Gearan** means 'complaint, concern'. The idea of care is 'anxiety, worry' and complain refers to pain or injury. Welsh *gera(i)n* is used of whining children.

gille – child. **Gille** means 'boy, lad'. The **ch** instead of **c** at the start of 'child' is surprising (English **ch** is frequently Gaelic **c**, see §4 above), but the Gaelic **ll** for English **ld** is normal (see §18).

gionach – chin. **Gionach** means 'greedy'. See §36.

glag – clack. **Glag** is 'a noise, thump'.

glaodh – clay. **Glaodh** is 'glue', which is another cognate. Glen Gloy near Spean Bridge is so called either because of its sticky clay soil or its sluggish river.

glas – clasp. **Glas** means 'a lock'. For the missing **p** in Gaelic see §20.

glùn – knee. Classical cognates are ge<u>nu</u>flect, and the various -gon compounds (penta<u>gon</u> etc). In the latter *gon* means angle, a reference to the bend of the knee. Gaelic **glùn** has **l** for the **n** of English (and other languages), an occasional feature of Modern Gaelic. So **A' Ghearmai<u>l</u>t** Germa<u>n</u>y, and **spùi<u>ll</u>** and **spùi<u>nn</u>**, both 'to plunder', mentioned below in §20.

gnàth(s) – know. **Gnàth** means 'custom, habit, usage'. The idea is 'what is known'. Classical cognates are 'gnostic, dia<u>gnose</u>, i<u>gno</u>rant' etc. For the vowel change from **à** to **o** see §31. The same root appears in **iongnadh** 'a wonder, something strange, surprising', with the negative prefix **ion** (English in-); in other words, 'not usual'. Also related is **gnothach** 'business'.

gnè – kind, kin, genus, genetic. **Gnè** means 'type, nature' A good example of the Gaelic treatment of the consonant vowel **n** mentioned in the introduction.

gràinne – corn. **Gràinne** is 'a grain, a small amount'. For the vowel change see again §34. Ballygrant, **Baile a' Ghràna**, in Islay, is thought to mean 'Grain Farmstead'.

greim – <u>chiro</u>practor and the many ch(e)iro compounds, all based on the Greek word for 'hand'. **Greim** means 'a hold, grip'. Typical Gaelic treatment of the consonant vowel **r**.

gruth – curd. The earlier English form was *crud*, as it still is in Scots (also spelled *croods*); compare also *crowdie*, a kind of brose.

gual – coal. For the vowel change see §38. The word appears in one or two placenames, but has **c** in their Gaelic spelling; so Collabol, **Colabol** 'Coal Farmstead' on the west side of Loch Shin, Sutherland. This is presumably due to the influence of Old Norse in such areas; the Norse form was *kol*, and the word order is Norse – Gaelic would have been **Baile Guail**.

gun – <u>cen</u>otaph. **Gun** means 'without'. A cenotaph is an empty tomb without a body. **Gun** had the form *cen* in Old Irish.

A couple of borrowings are:

gnog – knock. Borrowed from English or Scots when the **k** was still pronounced.

greideal – crate. **Greideal** is 'a griddle, gridiron'. Borrowed from Latin. For the English **t** but Gaelic **d** see §7.

As mentioned earlier, when **g** is not at the beginning of a Gaelic word it is sounded rather like English **c** (as in **c**at) or **k**. The following examples reflect this:

clag – clock. **Clag** is 'a bell'. Probably onomatopoeic. It is not clear whether clock (in its late Latin form *clocca*) was borrowed from Gaelic/Irish or vice-versa. **Clag** has **cluig** as its genitive, a form found in the diminutive **cluigean** 'little bell'. This word appears in the modern Gaelic **aol-chluigean** 'stalactite', a reference to the pendulous form of the limestone. Gaelic thus has the advantage of easily distinguishing between stalactites and stalagmites[20]. English, borrowing the words from Greek, doesn't distinguish between them etymologically, since both word mean 'drip, drop'; hence mnemonics such as 'mites up, tights down' – a reference to ants in the pants.

crog(an) – crock(ery). **Crog** and **crogan** mean 'a pitcher, an earthenware vessel'.

---

[20] A stalagmite is **aol-charragh** 'lime(stone) pillar'.

cuag – hook. See §2.

Dearg – dark. **Dearg** means 'red, crimson'.

deug – <u>dec</u>imal, <u>dec</u>ade etc. **Deug** is 'ten'.

e<u>asg</u>ann – Esk. **Easgann** is 'an eel', literally 'a water snake'. **Easg** is an obsolete word for a ditch, stream, cognate with river names such as Esk (Angus, Kincardine), Exe (England) and Usk (Wales).

fa<u>sg</u>adh – <u>sco</u>toma. **Fasgadh** means 'shelter', and scotoma is a blind spot in vision. The idea is one of shading from the light, making darker. **Fa** at the beginning of **fasgadh** is a preposition meaning 'under', like English '<u>sub</u>way'.

fusgan – whisk. **Fusgan** is 'a heather brush'.

iasg – Pisces. **Iasg** means 'a fish'. For the **p** of Pisces, the zodiac sign of the Fishes, missing in Gaelic see §20. 'Fish' is another cognate, with Indo-European **p** becoming **f** in English as mentioned under **uidh** in §7 above.

imleag – umbilical, omphalos, navel. **Imleag** means 'navel'. Indo-European **mb** becomes just **m** in modern Gaelic. Either of the letters may be dropped in various languages for ease of pronunciation, and their close association has meant that a **b**, for instance, is often added after **m** in English even if it doesn't belong to the word and shouldn't be there. So 'num**b**er' (but 'numeral'), 'thum**b**' and so on. Scots *nummer* and *thoom* get it right. The cognate 'navel' shows metathesis; the **m** of umbilical is due to the following **b**, and has become n when beginning the word. See also **imleag** §16.

lag – lax. **Lag** means 'weak'. The **x** in lax is, of course, the equivalent in sound of **ks.** 'Slack' is also cognate; English sometimes has an **s** at the start of a word where Latin (from which lax is borrowed) doesn't.[21] Also related is 'lang̲uid'; for the **n** missing in Gaelic see §19.

measg(aich) – mis̲c̲ellaneous, promis̲c̲uous. **Measgaich** means '(to) mix'. For the vowel change see §33.

meirg – murk, mirk. **Meirg** means 'rust'. The idea is a darkish, indistinct colour.

rag – rack. **Rag** means 'stiff, inflexible', slightly removed from 'rack' meaning 'stretch, strain'. Also related is 'rig̲id'.

seamrag – shamrock. The English is borrowed from Irish Gaelic.

seasg – desic̲c̲ated. **Seasg** means 'dry, barren'. For the vowel change see §33.

smug – mucus. **Smug** (more commonly **smugaid**) means 'a spit' (from the mouth). For the Gaelic initial **s** see §23.

uisge – whisky. **Uisge** means 'water', which is also cognate, as is Russian *vodka*. The English is borrowed from **uisge-beatha** 'water of life', the same idea as *aquavit*.

There are also a number of borrowings illustrating this feature:

adag – haddock. Borrowed from English. See also §16.

aigeann – ocean. Borrowed from Latin.

bagaid – bacca. **Bagaid** means 'a cluster', and 'bacca' is the botanical term for a berry; baccate means 'having bunches of berries'. Borrowed from Latin.

---

[21] Examples with **l** are 'slippery' and Latin *lubricus* (English 'lubricate') and 'slime' and Latin *limus*, 'lime', *limax* 'snail, slug'. English also has instances of related words of similar meaning with and without an initial **s**, 'lime' and 'slime' being examples. For instances in Gaelic see §23.

briogais – breeches, breeks. Borrowed from English.

briosgaid – biscuit. Borrowed from English.

brisgean – brisket. **Brisgean** is 'gristle, cartilage'. Borrowed from Norse.

Càisg – Paschal. **Càisg** is Easter; paschal is related to Passover, the Jewish festival occurring around the same time. For the Gaelic **c** for English **p** see §5. Borrowed from Latin.

caog – cock(eyed). **Caog** means '(to) wink'. Borrowed from English, but Scots *keek* may also be related.

ceangal – cingulum, cincture. **Ceangal** means 'tie, connect'. Borrowed from Latin.

cogall – cockle. This weed is also known as corncockle and tare. Borrowed from English.

crog – crock. Both words mean 'an old ewe', and the English (but not Gaelic) extends to horses, people and other decrepit things. Borrowed from Scots.

eaglais – <u>eccles</u>iastic. **Eaglais** means 'church'. Borrowed from Latin. Common in placenames, notably **An Eaglais Bhreac** (the Multi-coloured Kirk), Falkirk.

learag – larch, larick. The Gaelic is clearly borrowed from the Scots *larick*. It gives its name to Glenleraig, just west of Kylesku in Sutherland. Attempts to relate **learag** to **darach** on the strength of the d/l interchange mentioned under **teanga** §33 are untenable. There is no evidence that Latin and Greek *larix*, from which the English is ultimately borrowed, nor the Indo-European root, ever began with **d**. If it had, the English would be *tarch*.

mag – mock. Borrowed from English. For the change of vowel see §31.

margadh – market. Borrowed from English.

pèileag – pellack. Both words mean 'porpoise'. Pellack (also pellock and pellach) is Scots and may be the origin of the Gaelic.

pòg – pacify, peace. **Pòg** means 'kiss', the kiss of peace (*osculum pacis*) being part of church ritual at the time. From Latin *pax* 'peace', the standard classical meaning. In later ecclesiastical Latin *osculum* was dropped and *pax* by itself meant 'kiss', which explains the Gaelic. The vowel of *pax* was retained in the northern dialect of Gaelic and appears as **pàg** in the eighteenth-century poet Rob Donn's poem to Ann Morrison. Manx has *paag*.

rug – ruck. Both words mean 'a wrinkle'. Gaelic also has the more common form **ruc**. Borrowed from Norse. There also seems to be some sort of connection with the classical cognates 'rugose, corrugated'.

sagart – sacred, sacerdotal. **Sagart** means 'priest'. Borrowed from Latin. The word appears in a few placenames, as Auchentaggart (Sanquhar, Dumfries) and in the surnames Taggart, Haggart etc.

slìogach – sleekit. **Slìogach** means 'sly'. Borrowed from English or Scots.

snàig – sneak. **Snàig** means '(to) creep'. Probably borrowed from Scots, though the word is also cognate with English 'sneak, snake (crawler)'.

stang – stank. **Stang** means 'a pool, ditch'. Borrowed from Scots, where it currently means 'a gutter in the street', but ultimately from Latin. A classical cognate is 'stagnant'.

ùig – wick. Both words mean 'a bay, creek, inlet of the sea'. Borrowed from Norse *vik*, thought to be the origin of Viking, fiord people. Uig in Skye is just 'bay', and the word appears in the Gaelic version of some Scottish *wicks*; Wick in Caithness is **Inbhir Ùige**.

In the following words the **g** has been lenited, as explained in §12:

bloigh – block. **Bloigh** means 'a part, a piece, fragment'.

bragh – break, brick (a <u>broken</u> piece of clay). **Bragh** (also **braghadh**) means 'explosion'. The more usual word today, **spreagh**(**adh**) looks like an instance of **bragh** with an initial 'moveable' **s** (see §23), but is rather a borrowing from English 'spread' i.e. to scatter in all directions.

dogha – dock. **Dogha** means 'burdock', which is a dock with burs, prickly seed-heads.

eighe – axe. **Eighe** is 'a (metal) file' but also meant a peat cutter in parts of the West Highlands. Axe was *æx* in Old English, a bit nearer to the Gaelic vowels.

leagh – leak. **Leagh** means 'melt'.

nigh – nix(e). **Nigh** means 'wash'. *Nix(e)* is a male or female water spirit in Germanic mythology, usually unpleasant, which, with Old English *nicker* 'a water demon', has suggested a further connection with Nick, the devil. This male water spirit is commemorated in the Knucker Hole, a pool on the north edge of Lyminster, in England. Female water spirits, Nixies, gained a wider audience after Wagner's use of the word to describe the Rhinemaidens in his Ring cycle, and the word is now used (*Nixe*) in Germany as an imaginative registered trademark for fish products. Also cognate is <u>Nep</u>tune, the Roman god of the sea; Neptune's Staircase is a series of eight locks at the southern end of the Caledonian Canal, just outside Fort William.

sùgh – suck, <u>succ</u>ulent. **Sùgh** means 'juice'.

tiugh – thick. For the Gaelic **t** but English **th** see §28.

tràigh – re<u>tract</u>, con<u>tract</u>. **Tràigh** is 'a beach'. The idea is that of the sea drawing back, leaving the sandy beach exposed. So

tràghadh is 'ebbing'. The word occurs in many placenames, as Kentra, **Ceann Tràgha** 'Head of the Beach' a few miles north of Salen in Sunart; but the best known is probably **An Tràigh Mhòr** in the north of Barra, which serves as the island's aircraft landing strip.

Borrowings with this feature are:

conntraigh – contract(ion). **Conntraigh** is 'neap-tide', the smallest difference in tide levels. Thought to have been borrowed from Latin. For the Romans tides around Britain were a noted feature (compared with the Mediterranean), especially after the damage caused by the tide to the Channel fleet of Julius Caesar in 55 B.C. The ending -**traigh** 'beach' looks like a bit of folk etymology, though, as the previous entry indicates, it is cognate with the Latin.

leugh – <u>lec</u>tern. **Leugh** means '(to) read' and is borrowed from Latin. English keeps the **g** in 'legible, legend' etc.

saoghal – secular. **Saoghal** means 'world'. Borrowed from Latin. See also §32.

A special category of Gaelic **g** for English **c** or **k** occurs in the combination **sg** at the beginning of a word. This is because **sc** is not a permitted Gaelic combination – though it is in Irish, where **sg** is not found – and **k** is not a letter of the Gaelic alphabet, just as initial **sg** in not an English combination. Most examples are borrowings, and reflect spelling conventions in both languages, as indicated under several of the words below. As can be seen, English uses only **k** and not **c** if an **e** or **i** follows; this is because **c** is pronounced **s** when followed by these slender vowels (**c**ell, **c**ity), something which doesn't happen in Gaelic, **c** always being a hard **k** sound. Pure Gaelic cases are:

sgàird – scatological, sharn. **Sgàird** is 'diarrhoea', and sharn is a Scots word for cow dung.

sgath / English 'scathe'. **Sgath** means 'cut off, injure'. Scathing (i.e. 'cutting, wounding', used of remarks) and unscathed are in common use.

sgeallag – scilla. **Sgeallag** (also **sgeallan**) is 'wild mustard', and scilla (also squill) is a sea onion.

sgoilt – skill. **Sgoilt** means '(to) split, separate'. The original idea of 'skill' is discrimination, separateness, leading to the modern meaning of 'distinction'.

sgreuch / English 'screech'.

sgròb / English 'scrape' – **sgròb** means 'scratch'; for the Gaelic **b** for English **p** see §1.

Borrowings include:

sgainneal – scandal. Borrowed from Latin, as is the English. You can tell that the Gaelic is from Latin, rather than English, for various reasons. Firstly, the word appeared in written Irish in its so-called Middle Irish period (c.1200 to c.1600) when the English language was thin on the ground in Ireland. Secondly, the word represents a feature of Church belief at the time; it was used by the church to mean an impediment to faith, a discredit to religion. And the language of the Church was, of course, Latin. The modern Gaelic meaning of slander, malicious gossip etc is, however, from English, and in fact slander is just another form of scandal, coming into English from Old French. The Gaelic form reflects the replacement of **nd** by **nn** – see §19. Related is the surname Scanlon, originally describing someone who was argumentative and offensive.

sgait – skate (fish). Borrowed from English.

sgàld – scald. The Gaelic accent is there to reproduce the long vowel sound of the English from which it is borrowed.

sgàrlaid – scarlet. Borrowed from English or Latin. For the Gaelic **d** see §7.

sgeap – skep. Borrowed from Scots *skep*, 'a beehive' though the word is in earlier English and Old Norse. For the **a** in Gaelic see §34; the Gaelic **p** is also an indication that the word is borrowed, see §20. See also **beach** §33.

sgeir – skerry. Borrowed from Norse. For the **i** in Gaelic see §35. **An Sgeir Mhòr**, Skerryvore 'The big sea rock', off Mull, is a well-known lighthouse.

sgil – skill. Borrowed from English. Gaelic doesn't reproduce the double **l** of the English because **ll** with a slender vowel (**e** or **i**) in Gaelic has a sound like the **lli** in English 'million', particularly in the middle of a word. English, on the other hand, always has a double **l** at the end of monosyllables, but usually a single **l** if it's more than one syllable. So 'skill', but 'skilful', the double **l** making no difference to the sound, unlike in Gaelic.

sgiobair – skipper. Borrowed from English. For the Gaelic **b** see §1.

sgiort(a) – skirt. Borrowed from English. The Gaelic **o** is there because **i** occurs before **rt** only in combination with another vowel, either before (as **puirt**, 'ports') or after it, as here.

sgiùrs – scourge. Borrowed from English.

sgoil – school. Borrowed from Latin. The **i** is just there to reproduce the sound of English **l**, and certainly doesn't have the sound of the diphthong in English 'soil' etc. Gaelic **l** with a broad vowel (**a, o, u**) has a different sound from English, and since that's not what's wanted here, putting an **i** in gets the correct **l** sound.

sgòr – score (games, music). Borrowed from English. The accent is there to reproduce the long vowel sound of the English. English, unusually amongst the Germanic language family, uses an **e** <u>after</u> a consonant to change the sound of the preceding vowel; so for/fore, car/care and so on. Gaelic doesn't do this, but it formerly used grave and acute accents to distinguish the sounds of **e** and **o**. Nowadays only the grave is used, so you can't tell the precise sound of these vowels just by the accent.

sgrìobh – scribe, scribble. Borrowed from Latin. **Sgrìobh** means 'write'; the cognate 'script' shows Gaelic **b** for English **p**, see §1. From the same Latin root is **sgrìob**, 'scrape', again see §1.

sgriubha – a screw. Borrowed from English. The **bh** is not pronounced, but separates the vowels on either side, as often happens with borrowed words. **Bh** is a good choice in this instance, since it occurred in the Indo-European word from which 'screw' is derived, as seen in German *Schraube* – compare **cùmhnant** §38. The **a** is a faint neutral sound (compare **sgiort**(**a**) above) and in such instances is either an **e** or an **a** according to the spelling rule (see the end of the introduction).

sgrùd – scrutinise. Borrowed from Latin, as is the English. For the Gaelic **d** see §7.

sgùm – scum. Borrowed from Norse or Early English, both of which had a long vowel (unlike scum today), as does the Gaelic with its accent. This indicates an early borrowing, as of course many loanwords are, unlike **sgriubha** above.

§14 G AS ENGLISH H

A Gaelic **g** represents an English **h**, particularly at the start of a word. This goes back to Indo-European **gh,** which became **g** in some languages and **h** in others. Thus in English the word gar<u>d</u>en has a classical cognate '<u>hort</u>iculture' and bridegroom (i.e. bride man) should be bride<u>goom</u>[22] – hence the surname Gomme – and is cognate with the words <u>hom</u>o sapiens, <u>hom</u>icide etc. So Gaelic **geamhradh** 'winter' is related to English '<u>hiem</u>al' and '<u>Him</u>alaya(s)', hiemal being a classical cognate meaning 'wintry' and Himalaya(s) meaning 'snow-covered'. **Gamhainn** 'stirk, year-old calf' also has a reference to the onset of winter, as does **foghar** 'autumn', i.e. before winter. The **m** of **geamhradh** was there in earlier Irish *fogamur* (modern Irish *fómhar*) and Gaelic **foghar** is often pronounced with a **v** sound in the middle of the word in some areas.

This **g/h** interchange has echoes elsewhere; Dutch **g** is pronounced **gh** (like a Gaelic **gh**) and Welsh **g** when mutated has no sound at all, not even **h** (a simple **h** sound often disappears in languages, as frequently heard in the colloquial English of southern England – (h)orse, (h)ouse etc).

Other words with this feature are:

garbh – <u>hir</u>sute. **Garbh** means 'rough'.

gart – <u>hort</u>iculture. **Gart** is 'a cornfield, standing corn'. Also cognate is 'garden'. In its general meaning of 'field' the word is found in quite a number of placenames, as Gartocharn, **Gart a' Chàirn** 'Field of the Cairn' at the south end of Loch Lomond.

---

[22] The **r** inserted later is probably a bit of folk etymology based on the separate word *groom*.

gas – <u>has</u>tate. **Gas** means 'a stalk, twig', and hastate is a botanical term referring to spear-shaped stalks and leaves. For the Gaelic loss of **t** see §22.

goirtean – <u>hor</u>ticulture. **Goirtean** 'small field' is a diminutive of **gart** above. It occurs in a few placenames, as Gortan, a few miles west of Strathpeffer, Ross & Cromarty.

§15 G AS ENGLISH GN

In Gaelic **g** disappears before **n** inside a word,[23] but is retained in English. So **uan** 'lamb' is cognate with *agnus*. *Agnus* is Latin but is familiar from church use, as *agnus dei* 'lamb of God'. The loss of the **g** in Gaelic is echoed in French and Italian (*agneau*, *agnello*, both 'lamb') where the **g** is written but not sounded, though it affects the sound of the following **n**. Other instances are:

feun – wagon. The Old English form was *waegn*. See also under **feun** §9.

MacMhànais (MacManus) – Magnusson. All words are based on the Latin *magnus* 'great', with the Gaelic showing loss of **g** but the Norse retaining it. Another surname form, Manson, is a mixture – no **g**, so Gaelic-influenced, but *-son*, so Norse.

seun – sign (with its various prefixes), signature, signal, toc<u>sin</u>. Borrowed from Latin. **Seun** means 'a charm, a good-luck sign'. The **g** isn't sounded in English 'sign' either, echoing Romance language pronunciation of Latin **gn**, as mentioned under **uan** above. The adjective **seunta** 'charmed, enchanted' appears in Loch Seunta 'Holy Loch' in Cowal, and in the Shiant Isles east of Harris.

---

[23] But not at the beginning. There are quite a few words starting with **gn**, though the usual pronunciation is **gr**.

§16 LOSS OF INITIAL H

In Gaelic the letter **h** is mainly used as a sign of lenition, to change the sound of a consonant, and doesn't really count as a letter in its own right. It is not found at the beginning of a genuine Gaelic word, though it does appear there in some modern borrowings, as **hama**, 'ham', **hocaidh**, 'hockey' and so on. But in many words borrowed from other languages Gaelic has dropped the **h**, as **ad**, 'hat'. Some other instances are:

abharsaic – haversack. Borrowed from English.

adag – haddock. Borrowed from English. See also §13.

Eabhra – Hebrew. Borrowed from Latin.

Eanraig – Henry. Borrowed ultimately from Latin.

(an) Eilbheis – Helvetia. Borrowed from Latin. Helvetia is now called Switzerland, but the name still survives - for instance on postage stamps and in Confederatio Helvetica (CH), the International Vehicle Registration for Switzerland.

èiteag – hectic. **Èiteag** means 'pebble'; the more usual form today is **dèideag**, where the **d** belonged originally to the article. See also **deigh** §42. This happens in English with the indefinite article, as words like (n)adder, (n)apron, (n)ewt, (n)umpire etc show. A hectic stone was the name given to a pebble supposedly effective against fevers and various other illnesses, hectic being an old name for a fever. Borrowed from English.

òb – hope. Both words mean 'a bay', and in both languages appear in placenames, as St Margaret's Hope (Orkney) and Oban, **An t- Òban** 'The Little Bay'. Borrowed from Norse. See also §1.

oighre – heir. The unpronounced initial **h** in the English reflects the Latin spelling, from which the English, and possibly the

LOSS OF INITIAL H

Gaelic, come. The Gaelic **gh** is simply there to separate the vowels and has no sound.

(**an**) **Òlaind** – Holland. Gaelic follows English in loosely using the province Holland to mean the Netherlands.

onair – honour. Borrowed from Latin. The unpronounced initial **h** in the English reflects the Latin spelling.

osan – hose (sock, stocking). Borrowed from English.

òsta – host. Usually found in the combination **taigh-òsta** 'hotel, inn'. Also cognate are 'hotel' and 'hostel', 'hospice' and 'hospital'. Borrowed from English.

uair – hour. Borrowed from Latin, which again accounts for the initial **h** in English.

umha(i)l – humble. Its meaning today is mainly 'obedient'. Borrowed from Latin. The **b** in English is not really part of the word - compare the related 'humiliate' - but has been added (both in English and in French, from which English borrowed it) for reasons of euphony. But even if Gaelic had borrowed it from English it wouldn't have kept the **b**, since **mb** is not a modern Gaelic combination[24] – Indo-European **mb** simply becomes **m** in Gaelic. Hence **òmar** 'amber', a borrowing from English. See also **imleag** §13.

(**an**) **Ungair** – Hungary. Borrowed from English.

---

[24] Unless the letters belong to two separate words, as **Caimbeul** 'Campbell', from **cam** and **beul**.

There are also a couple of instances of this feature in original Gaelic words:

aileag – in<u>ha</u>le, halitosis. **Aileag** means 'hiccup', which can be described as a slight (hence the Gaelic diminutive **-ag** ending) involuntary breathing in.

àirneis – harness. **Àirneis** means 'furniture' in modern Gaelic, but the general meaning is that of 'equipment'.

§17 L AS ENGLISH L

In words borrowed from English and other languages Gaelic frequently inserts an **i** before an **l** in order to make the Gaelic word sound more like the borrowed one. Usually this means that the Gaelic dark or back **l**, a quite distinctive sound which occurs when **l** is next to a broad vowel (**a**, **o**, **u**), is avoided. Sometimes there is no broad vowel involved, but Gaelic doesn't allow the letter **e** to stand before **l**, so **i** is inserted after the **e**. In many cases the inserted **i** has a slight sound and in some areas affects the sound of the preceding vowel. So **cailc**, 'chalk' has the English cognate 'ca<u>lc</u>ium'; contrast this with another borrowed word, **calc** 'caulk', where the sound of the **l** is quite different.

Other instances of this feature are:

<u>**cail**</u>**leach** – pall. See **cailleach** §5. Borrowed ultimately from Latin.

ceilp – kelp. The origin of this word is obscure, but the **p** indicates that Gaelic has borrowed it. Here the **i** has been inserted because the form *celp* is not allowed, as mentioned above.

coilear – collar. Borrowed from English. The slender vowels of the Gaelic avoid a dark **l**, and so a single **l** is then required to get the correct sound – see under **peileir** below.

dail – dale. Borrowed from Norse or English.

dèilig – deal (with). Borrowed from English. The **i** inserted as in **ceilp** above.

èildear – elder (of the Kirk). Borrowed from English.

pailm – palm (tree). Borrowed from Latin or English.

peileir – pellet. **Peileir** (or **peilear**) is commonly used today to mean 'bullet'. Ultimately from Latin *pila*, 'a ball', but borrowed through French at a later stage. Gaelic doesn't have the double **l** of pellet since that would give a **ly** sound, which is not what's required here. Such a sound applies only with slender vowels (**e** and **i**), so in another borrowing, **Nollaig**, the pronunciation is roughly *nolek*. **Nollaig**, 'Christmas', borrowed from Latin, is related to 'natal', referring to the birth of Christ. This time Gaelic has the double **l**, though there appears to be no reason for it with this particular word. Nor with **Callainn**, 'New Year's Day', English cognates 'calends' and 'calendar', since there is only one **l** in the Latin word from which both the Gaelic and English are borrowed. Calends is the first day of the month. Contrast **galan**, 'gallon', borrowed from English.

sgoil – school. See §13.

tàillear – tailor. The Gaelic double **l** suggests that it was borrowed from Scots *tailyour*, attested as early as the 15th century and only recently obsolete.

tràill – thrall. Borrowed from Norse or English. English prefers the word 'slave' (from the frequently conquered Slavs), but Gaelic has stuck with the earlier[25] borrowing.

An interesting reflection of this can be seen in the many placenames using the word **baile** 'town(ship), farm settlement' etc – a place with buildings. In fact **baile** is related to English 'build'; for the loss of **d** after **l** in Gaelic see §18 (though it usually results in a Gaelic double **l**). **Baile** is almost invariably anglicised as *bal* or *ball*, following the Gaelic pronunciation. So Balallan, **Baile Ailein** 'Alan's Township', Ballachulish, **Baile a' Chaolais** 'Settlement at the Narrows' and so on.

---

[25] 'Thrall' is first attested in about 950, but it is more than three centuries later before 'slave' appears.

§18 LL AS ENGLISH LD, LT AND SL

A Gaelic double **l** represents an English **ld**, **lt** or **sl**. This is a form of assimilation because the **d** and **t** are assimilated back (forward in the case of **s**) to the **l**, so a double **l** occurs. This is a feature of many languages; in English, the negative prefix *in-* (e.g. inactive) appears also as illegal, immodest, irregular etc with the ***n*** assimilated to the following letter. Gaelic instances relating to **ld** are:

geall – guild. **Geall** means 'a wager, prize', and guild (also spelled *gild*) is related to Old English *gield* 'an offering'. So also cognate is 'yield' (a profit, income); for the **y** see §12.

gille – child. **Gille** means 'a boy, lad', and historically, 'a servant'. The problem is that 'child' has its origin in an Indo-European word for womb, and **gille** is restricted to males. For the Gaelic **g** see §13. The word occurs in surnames such as Gillespie, Gilchrist, Gillies, Gilmore etc with the meaning 'servant', and in a few placenames, as **Sgùrr nan Gillean**, a famous peak on Skye.

moll – mould, moulder (to turn to dust). **Moll** means 'chaff, dust', and Scots has forms of 'mould' without the **d**. Also cognate is 'mole'. Mole is thought to be a contraction of mouldwarp, a reference to the creature's habit of throwing up small heaps of earth.

Instances relating to **lt** are:

call – halt. See §2.

coille – holt. See §2.

saill – (to) salt. Classical cognates are 'salad, salary, saline' etc.

An instance relating to **sl** is **call** – hazel. See §2 under **calltainn.**

§19 NN AS ENGLISH ND AND NT

Like **l** in §12 double **n** appears in place of English **nd** and **nt**. Instances of the former are:

ainneamh – <u>und</u>omesticated. **Ainneamh** means 'scarce, rare'. The **d** appears in Early Irish *andam*; the idea is 'not homely', i.e. not familiar.

ainnir – anther, anthology. **Ainnir** means 'virgin', and anther is part of the stamen of a flower. All the antho- compounds in English come from the Greek word for flower; the idea of **ainnir** is 'not deflowered'.

bonn – <u>found</u>(ation), <u>fund</u>ament. **Bonn** means 'the base, sole, foundation'. Gaelic initial **b** sometimes represents English **f**, as **blàth** 'blossom, bloom', cognate with 'flower', **bràthair** 'brother' and 'fraternal', **bile(ag)** 'leaf' cognate with 'folio, foliage', **beirm** 'yeast' (borrowed from English barm) and '<u>ferment</u>' etc (which last is also found in the cognate **to<u>bar</u>** 'a well' (i.e. a welling up). **Tobar** is common in placenames, as Tobermory, **Tobar Mhoire** 'Mary's Well' on Mull. **Bonn** may also be the root of **o<u>bann</u>** 'sudden'; compare the phrase **an làrach nam bonn** 'immediately'. Also related is **fonn** 'land', see below.

cràin – grunt. **Cràin** is 'a sow'. A double **n** might have been expected in the Gaelic but the accent may be compensatory. In any case the words are onomatopoeic.

fionn – <u>Find</u>horn. **Fionn** means 'white, fair' and Findhorn 'white Eren' is a village in Morayshire, Eren being a local river. The form Findhorn shows the insertion of **d** in surnames and placenames, a feature of Scots, as Fin**d**lay, Hen**d**ry. This intrusive **d** has also become a feature of English; words such as sound, lend, thunder etc appeared in earlier English without the **d** and this earlier form is really the correct one, as related cognates show, as, for instance, Scots *len* 'a loan'.

fonn – sound. **Fonn** means 'a tune'. For the initial Gaelic **f** but English **s** see §11.

lann – land. The word has rather fallen out of use, but appears in the word **iodhlann** 'cornyard'. But as usual it is found in placenames, as Echline 'Horse Land', South Queensferry, West Lothian, and in Gaelic forms of English placenames, as **Fàclann**, Falkland 'Falcon Land' in Fife. It also appears in the name **Lachlann**, Lochlann i.e. (sea)loch land, a forename and surname as well as the Gaelic name for Scandinavia. So the final **d** disappears in other countries given a Gaelic form more recently, as **a' Phòlainn** (Polan_d_) and **Fionnlann** (Finlan_d_), probably influenced also by traditional **Èirinn** (Ireland) and **Sasann** (England). **Lann** is cognate with the very common Welsh *llan*, 'church(yard)', this form appearing in a few placenames in this country also, as Lhanbryde 'St Bride's Church', in Moray.

mannas – man_d_ible. **Mannas** (also **bannas**) is 'the gum' (dental) and mandible is a jaw(bone). Related is **manntach** 'stuttering'.

teann – dis_tend_. **Teann** means 'tight, tense'.

Borrowings with this feature are:

bann – band, bandage. Borrowed from English.

beannachd – bene_dict_ion. Borrowed from Latin, giving rise to the surnames Benedict and Bennett. See also §6 and §34.

coinneal – candle. Borrowed from Latin.

fonn – _fund_amental, foun_d_(ation). **Fonn** is 'land, domain', seldom used today. Borrowed from Latin *fundus*, 'farm, estate'. Fonab in Perthshire is **Fonn an Aba** 'the Abbot's Land'.

Lunnainn – London. The word was often pronounced in earlier centuries without the **d** in English too.

sainnseal – handsel. Borrowed from English or Scots. See also §25.

sgainneal – scandal. Borrowed from Latin. See also §13.

uinneag – window. Borrowed from Norse.

An instance with **nt** is **clann**, which is cognate with 'plant', referring to propagation, seed. **Clann** means 'children' and is the origin of 'clan'. For the *c/p* interchange see §5.

Sometimes, however, Gaelic drops **n** before certain consonants, namely **c**, **g**, **s**, and **t**; for the last see the end of §7. Instances with **c** (or **k**) in the English are:

eug – ne<u>cro</u>polis. **eug** means 'death, die' and a necropolis is a cemetery (city of the dead). The now missing Gaelic **n** was after the **e** (the earlier hypothetical form being *enk*- or similar), and is still there in Welsh *angau*, which, like Gaelic, shows metathesis from the *nec*- form found in Latin, Greek (from which come the various necro- compounds in English) and other languages. So this metathesis took place at an early stage in the Celtic languages, and may be related to the Indo-European **n** as a consonant vowel, mentioned in the introduction. But the process is also more recent in Gaelic, as **nighean** 'girl, daughter' from earlier **inghean**[26] illustrates, though it is also possible that the initial **i** has dropped off when it was no longer stressed.

leig – re<u>lin</u>quish. **Leig** means 'let go, leave'. The **q** of 'relinquish' is, of course, simply the English spelling convention for **cw** or **kw**. Also related is **dìll<u>eachd</u>an** 'orphan', i.e. someone left.

---

[26] This earlier form, still the norm in Irish, is thought to be the source of the female name Imogen, first found in Shakespeare's *Cymbeline* and presumed to be a misreading of an earlier Innogen 'girl'.

NN AS ENGLISH ND AND NT

màg – e<u>manc</u>ipate. **Màg** means 'a paw, a hand', and is found in Scots *maig* (various spellings). The idea of emancipate is 'to unhand'.

And borrowings are:

acair – anchor. Ultimately from Latin via Norse. Acair is a well-known publishing company of Gaelic-related material based in Stornoway, Lewis.

bac – bank. **Bac** usually refers to a peat bank, and occurs in the placename Back in Lewis. Borrowed from Norse.

spìocach – pinch. **Spìocach** means 'miserly, niggardly' and pinch has the sense of 'stint, be sparing with'. See also §23 for the 'movable' initial **s**, and for English as a possible source of the borrowing.

Instances with **g** in the English are:

lag – languid. **Lag** means 'weak, faint'.

òg – young. The source of the surname Ogg (=Young), which retains the long vowel of the Gaelic, and was earlier spelled with a single **g.**

Instances with **s** in the English are:

gleus – glance. **Gleus** means 'good condition', with the idea of 'cleaned up, shiny'. Glance is a mineral with a metallic sheen, and glance-coal is another name for anthracite. The **c** has the sound of **s**, of course.

meas – mense. **Meas** means 'respect, esteem', as does the Scots *mense*. The word appears also in **tomhas** 'measurement, weight' and **dìmeas** 'disrespect'.

mìos – mens(u)al. **Mìos** means 'month', another cognate. For the vowel change see §36.

Here also may belong **bàs** – bane. **Bàs** means 'death'. For the missing **s** in English 'bane' compare 'month' (under **mìos** in the previous entry), which has lost the **s**. The traditional explanation refers to English cognates batter, beat, battle etc, deriving from a Celtic root *ba-*, but this doesn't explain the **s** of **bàs**. But baste (to thrash) and bash, both probably of Scandinavian origin, show an **s** which may account for the Gaelic form. Ardvasar **Àird a' Bhàsair**, a village and promontory in Sleat peninsula, Skye, may have some reference to a long-forgotten disaster there.

Borrowings include:

cìs – census. **Cìs** means 'tax'. Borrowed from Latin. For the vowel change see §36.

mias – mensal. **Mias** means 'a dish', and mensal means 'relating to the table'. Also related is Mensa, Table, a constellation in the southern hemisphere. Borrowed from Latin.

pòs – <u>spons</u>al, <u>spons</u>or. **Pòs** means 'marry, wed'. Other cognates are 'spouse, espousal' etc. The basic idea is 'promise'. For the initial **s** missing in Gaelic see §23. Borrowed from Latin.

§20 Loss of P

This is not, as a rule, an original Gaelic letter, though it is found in a few words beginning **sp-**; the **p** in such instances was sometimes written earlier as **b**, but initial **sb** is no longer a permitted combination in Gaelic. There are also a very few words such as **streap** '(to) climb', which don't seem to be borrowed and so are presumably native Gaelic; the **p** in such cases is thought to be the result of an earlier combination of letters. Generally, though, **p** will be missing from Gaelic words but present in many of their English cognates. In some of these English has **f**, or its voiced equivalent **v**, in place of the missing Gaelic **p**. Such instances are:

aitheamh – fathom. The letter **p** appears in the cognate 'patent' (spread out); a fathom was originally the distance between the outstretched arms, now six feet.

alt – fold. **Alt** means 'a joint'. For the vowel change see §31.

athair – father. A classical cognate is 'paternal', and the various patri- and patron- compounds, as well as the more modern 'patter'. This last refers to glib and rapid speech, from Latin *pater* *noster* (our father), the opening of the Lord's Prayer, the prayer allegedly being rattled through by priests.

cuan – haven. **Cuan** nowadays means 'sea, ocean', but used to mean 'harbour' – see §2 for this and the initial **c**. For the missing **v** in Gaelic see §30.

iasg – fish. A classical cognate is Pisces, the Fishes sign of the Zodiac. The **p** remains in the related gram*pus* (fat fish), and por*poise* (pig fish).

ite – feather. For the Gaelic **i** see §36 – feather was earlier *fether*.

làr – floor. For the vowel change see §31.

leathann – flat. **Leathann** means 'broad'. Cognates with **p** are 'plat, plate, plateau, platform, platypus' etc. Fairly common in placenames, as Broadford **An t-Àth Leathann** in Skye, and Glen Lean in Cowal.

liath – fallow. **Liath** is 'grey' and fallow means 'brownish' (the colour of deer). See also **liath** below.

luath – fleet, float. **Luath** means 'swift'.

seachd – seven. The **p** occurs in words such as septet.

uidh – foot. **Uidh** is 'a journey'. See also below in this section.

uircean – farrow. **Uircean** is 'a piglet'. See also below in this section.

Slightly unusual, because of the initial **p**, is the relationship between **preas** and furze. **Preas** is a general term for a bush, and furze is another word for gorse and whin. The **p** indicates a borrowing, in this instance thought to be from Pictish/Old British.

More simple instances with just the missing **p** are:

aire – experience. **Aire** means 'notice, attention'.

at – patent. **At** means '(to) swell'. The idea is 'open, distended, spread out'.

caor – carpal, polycarpic. **Caor** means 'berry', particularly that of the rowan (**caorann**). Carpel is the reproductive element of a flower, and polycarpic means 'bearing much fruit'.

caora – capric, caprid, Capricorn. **Caora** means 'a sheep'; capri- compounds refer to goats. Such changes happen in different languages; in Greek *kapros* is 'a boar'. This feature occurs even within the Celtic languages; Gaelic **damh** 'stag, ox' is cognate with Welsh *dafad* 'sheep'.

drùchd – drop, drip. **Drùchd** is 'dew'. For the letters **chd** in place of **p** see **feasgar**, **seachd** and **uachdar** below in this section.

eas – ped- compounds (pedestal etc). **Eas** is 'a waterfall', and the idea is 'downwards, to the foot', foot being the sense, as well as a cognate, of ped- compounds. The word is common in placenames, as Bunessan **Bun Easain**, 'the Foot of the Little Waterfall', in the Ross of Mull.

<u>eidheann</u> – im<u>pede</u>. **Eidheann** is 'ivy'. The original meaning of impede in its Latin form, from which English borrowed it, was 'to shackle, restrict the feet of'. There are many ped- compounds in English from this root of 'foot' (pedal etc), but native English 'fetter' is another cognate; its literal meaning is to shackle by the <u>feet</u>. (Contrast 'manacle' under **muinichill** §42). For the English **f** for Indo-European **p** see **uidh** §7. The idea, of course, is that ivy is shackled or bound to trees, walls etc. The word appears in a few placenames, as Camasine **Camas Eidhinn**, 'Ivy Bay' on the north shore of Loch Sunart, Argyll.

eun – pen. **Eun** means 'bird', and pen has basic meaning of 'feather, quill', and hence now a writing instrument using ink.

glas – clasp. **Glas** means 'a lock'. See also §13.

iall – pile. **Iall** is 'a thong, shoelace' and pile is a piece of yarn, a hair.

làmh – palm, palama. **Làmh** means 'hand'. Palama is the webbing on the feet of ducks etc.

làn – plenty, re<u>plen</u>ish. **Làn** means 'full'. See also **liuthad** below.

leac – lapidary, lapis lazuli; plaque, plack. **Leac** is 'a stone slab'. It's not certain whether the missing **p** is internal, as found in the first two English instances (which relate to stone), or initial, as in the last two (which relate to a flat object, usually metal). A plack is an old Scottish coin. See also §34.

liath – pallid, pale. **Liath** means 'grey, slate-coloured'. Also cognate is 'fallow', see under **liath** above. For the Monadhliath mountains see **monadh** §42.

lios – place. **Lios** is 'a garden', i.e. a flat wide area. The Argyll island Lismore **Lios Mòr** is 'the Big Garden' because of its fertile soil, and the word occurs in England also, as Liss, Liskeard etc, where the meaning is 'courtyard'.

lite – poultice, pulse. **Lite** is 'porridge', which is, of course, made from cereals, not pulses, but the reference is to the cooked dish.

liuthad – plus. **Liuthad** means 'so many'. Also related are the various plen- compounds – see **làn** above.

loth – pullet, polecat. **Loth** is a colt, a young horse of either sex. A pullet is, of course, a hen; in Latin, from which the word ultimately comes, it means both a young horse and other animals and birds, as well as a hen. The related Welsh *llwdn* means 'a chicken' among other young creatures. A polecat is thought to be so-called because it frequently attacked hens.

òl – potable, potion. **Òl** means '(to) drink'. The accent over the **ò** suggests a compensatory lengthening due to a disappearing consonant, something which happens regularly in Gaelic (and other languages). The English cognates indicate that in Indo-European this consonant was **t**, a view strengthened by the fact that Welsh retains the **t** (or rather its voiced form **d**) in such related words; **sgeul** 'story', mentioned below in this section, is Welsh *chwedl*. All of this makes the suggested connection of **òl** with English *ale* unlikely, particularly since ale is related to the plant alum.

othar – putrid. **Othar** is 'an abscess, ulcer'. Also related is **òtrach**, the next entry.

òtrach – putrid. **Òtrach** means 'a dung-heap, midden', and **a' bhreac-òtraich** is chickenpox. The word is found occasionally in placenames, as Auchnotroch, **Achadh nan Òtrach** 'Field of the Middens' at Lesmahagow, and similarly Auchnotteroch in Wigtownshire. For the vowel change see §37.

riamh – <u>prim</u>itive. **Riamh** means 'before, ever, in the past'.

ro – <u>pro</u>logue. **Ro** means 'before', as does the prefix *pro* in English. Also cognate are *fore* and *from* with the initial **f** for **p** as mentioned under **ùidh** §7. **Ro** was formerly written **roimh**, which better matches the cognate *fro<u>m</u>*.

ros – <u>prost</u>ate. **Ros** is 'a promontory', found today mainly in placenames, as Ross itself; modern words are **rubha**, **sròn** and **àird**, the last appearing tautologically in Ardrossan. The idea is 'standing in front'; the prostate gland stands in front of the bladder. For the missing **t** in Gaelic see §22.

saor – sapid, sapient. **Saor** is 'a joiner', and sapid and sapient mean 'wise, knowledgeable, discerning'. The idea is that carpentry and other trades (**saor** had a wider meaning earlier) are skilled crafts. Ardersier, **Àird nan Saor** 'Promontory of the Carpenters' is a few miles west of Nairn. The surname MacIntyre, **Mac an t-Saoir** means 'Son of the Joiner', and the Cornish name Sayer refers to carpentry.

sealg – spleen, splanchnic. **Sealg** means 'spleen, milt, soft roe (of fish)' and splanchnic is a classical cognate meaning 'intestinal, visceral'.

sine – spean. **Sine** is 'a nipple, teat' and *spean* (various spellings) is a Scots word meaning 'to wean'. The idea is privative, i.e. to disuse, remove from normal usage, as, for instance, Scots *heid* (behead).

sionn – spink. **Sionn** is an old Irish word for foxglove, and **sionnach** is modern Gaelic for 'a fox', though its etymology is unclear. Spink describes several kinds of flower, as lady's smock, primrose etc, but the etymology of the word is uncertain; it may be a form of 'pink', also used of various flowers. For the initial **s** see §23. Modern Gaelic for foxglove is **lus nam ban-sìth** 'flower of the fairies, (although, as in English, there are other local names), reflecting the fact that foxglove is possibly really 'folks' glove', folk being 'the little people', elves, pixies etc. Gaelic specifies female fairies (**ban-sìth** – banshee), which is quite appropriate since flowers frequently have a female name – lady's-, maiden's – etc, compared with fewer male references.

sir – speir. **Sir** means 'search for', and speir, now confined to Scots, means 'to ask about'. Related also is spoor 'search after, track'.

slis – splice, slice. **Slis** is 'a chip, wood shaving'.

suain – sopor, hy<u>p</u>notise. **Suain** means 'deep sleep'. For the Gaelic **s** but English **h** (in hypnotise) see §24.

teth – tepid. **Teth** means 'hot'. Related are **teine** 'fire' and **teas** 'heat'.

uasal – hy<u>p</u>sometry. **Uasal** means 'noble, high-born', and hypsometry is the measurement of heights. Related, from early British, are the Ochil Hills. The Scots word *duni<u>w</u>assal* (various spellings) 'gentleman', borrowed from Gaelic, also contains **uasal**.

uchd – <u>pec</u>toral. **Uchd** means 'breast'.

uidh – <u>pod</u>ium, <u>pod</u>agra. **Uidh** is 'a journey, stage' (originally on foot). Podagra is gout in the foot. For the vowel change see §38.

uile – poly-. **Uile** means 'all, every'. For the vowel change see §38. It is possible, however, that **uile** is related instead to English 'all'.

<u>**uir**</u>**cean** – pork. **Uircean** means 'piglet'. See also above in this section and for the vowel change see §38.

ulbhach – <u>pulv</u>erise. **Ulbhach** is 'ashes', a Badenoch word, now rare. Pulverise means to reduce to dust, but Latin *pulvis*, from which the English comes, was also used to mean the ashes of the cremated dead, Horace's *pulvis et umbra sumus* 'we are but dust and shadow'.

ùr – pure. **Ùr** means 'new, fresh'. It occurs in several placenames indicating recent settlements, **baile ùr** being the equivalent of English *Newton*, as for instance **Baile Ùr an t-Slèibh**, Newtonmore in Inverness-shire. It is possible, however, that **ùr** may be cognate with hygro- compounds in English, meaning 'moist, wet', as hygroscope, a device for recording air humidity. For the absence of **g** see §15.

Borrowings can also show this feature, as **baist** – baptise (for the metathesis see §40) and **salm** – psalm. Both borrowed from Latin, though of Greek origin. **Ulag** 'pulley', from English, seems to be another example.

There are a few instances where **p** in English has become a guttural (**ch, g**) in Gaelic, as:

feasgar – vesper(s). **Feasgar** means 'afternoon, evening'. For the Gaelic **f** see §9.

seachd – septet. **Seachd** is 'seven'. For the Gaelic **d** see §7.

uachdar – upper. Usually anglicised as Ochter (e.g. Drumochter on the A9 south of Dalwhinnie) or Auchter (e.g. Auchtermuchty in Fife), but there is also simple An t-Uachdar in Benbecula.

§21 S AS ENGLISH F

An initial **s** in Gaelic sometimes represents an English **f** in words borrowed from Latin. Briefly, the reason for this is that Irish in its earliest stage had no **f** sound. Later, when lenition developed, words starting with an **sv** or **sw** sound were lenited to **f-** (**f** being an unvoiced **v**). Thus a native word like *svesor* 'sister' (which later became *siur*) was lenited as *fiur*[27].

This meant that in Early Irish, borrowed words beginning with an **f** were subconsciously regarded as lenited versions of an **s-** word, and this **s-** form became the normal unlenited form. So **sòrn** relates to furnace; **sòrn** means 'flue' (of a kiln), as does Scots *sornie*, borrowed from Gaelic. For the vowel change see §37. The word for furnace is **fùirneis**, borrowed from English. Furnace, **An Fhùirneis**, is a village on the north shore of Loch Fyne, the site of ironworks in the late 18th and early 19th centuries. Other instances of this feature are:

sleuchd – genuflect, flex. **Sleuchd** means 'kneel'.

spong – fungus. **Spong** means 'tinder', sponge being a type of easily combustible tinder. For the vowel change see §37.

srian – fr(a)enum, refrain. **Srian** means 'a bridle', and frenum is a medical term for any supporting or restraining ligament in the human body. 'Refrain' had the original meaning of restraining by means of a bridle.

sroghall – flagellate. **Sroghall** means 'a whip', though the word is now obsolete, **cuip** or **sgiùrsair** – both borrowed from English – being used instead. The interchange of **r** (**sroghall**) and **l**

---

[27] Gaelic later took this a step further, once it had acquired the **p** sound. Irish fiur was regarded as a lenited form (*phiur* – same sound as *fiur*), and so the normal unlenited form became **piuthar** 'sister'. The internal t was part of the Indo-European and Celtic stem, and appears in the cognate 'sister'.

(f̲lagellate) is an occasional feature of Gaelic; many readers may recall the well-known song **Griogal Cridhe**, where **Griogal** is a variant of **Griogair** 'Gregor'. Likewise **Màili** and **Màiri**. See also **eileatrom** §10.

suaineadh – fu̲ni̲cle, fu̲ni̲cular. **Suaineadh** is 'twisting like a rope, entwining' and funicle is a cord, rope. In all such borrowings Welsh retains the Latin **f** and the Welsh word in question here would be *ffunen*, now 'a narrow ribbon of cloth, a band'. But there is also the possibility that **suaineadh** may be an original Gaelic word from an Indo-European root *sogn* or similar (for the missing **g** in Gaelic see §15) and there are plenty of modern European cognates for this. So there is some uncertainty.

sùist – fustigate. **Sùist** is 'a flail', and fustigate means '(to) beat, cudgel'.

§22 S AS ENGLISH ST AND KS

Some Gaelic words ending in **s** have lost a final **t**, while others have lost **c** before the **s** compared with their English cognates. In the latter case the English word is usually written with **x**, which, of course, has the sound of **ks**. Examples of the former (missing **t**) are:

àros – rest. **Àros** is 'a house', or 'apartments in a building' – somewhere to stay. The initial **à** of the Gaelic is a prefix with the sense of 'at'.

cas – haste. **Cas** means 'steep, rapid, sudden'. For the Gaelic **c** but English **h** see §2.

cluas – <u>list</u>en. **Cluas** means 'ear'. See §2 again.

fàs – vast, waste(land). **Fàs** means 'empty, vacant'. For the Gaelic **f** see §9.

gas – <u>hast</u>ate. **Gas** means 'a stalk, twig', and the botanical term hastate describes a pointed leaf. For the Gaelic **g** see §14.

ros – prostate. **Ros** is 'a promontory'. See **ros** §20.

seas – sist. **Seas** means '(to) stand, stop', and sist is a legal term with the same meaning. See also §33.

Examples with the missing **k** sound are:

às – ex. **As** means 'from, out of', and *ex* is the Latin preposition of similar meaning commonly used in English as a prefix (<u>ex</u>clude etc) or standing on its own (ex-directory etc).

cas – coxa. **Cas** means 'leg, foot', and coxa is 'the hip'. For the vowel change see §31. There is also a possible connection with 'hose', i.e. stockings etc; for the English **h** see §2.

deas – <u>dex</u>ter. **Deas** means 'right (hand), south'. See also §34.

S AS ENGLISH ST AND KS

fàs – wax. **Fàs** means 'grow, increase'. For the initial **f** see §10.

os – ox. **Os** means 'elk, moose'. Also cognate is the extinct *aurochs*. For the change of meaning see **caora** §20. This is possibly the meaning of Ben Oss a few miles west of Crianlarich.

A borrowed instance is:

crois – crux. **Crois** is 'a cross', borrowed from Latin, and English 'crux', usually meaning 'a difficulty, a critical issue of a problem', comes from the use of a small cross-like symbol in printing. Gaelic **crois** has adopted this meaning also. For the vowel change see §37.

§23 MOVEABLE S

Some Gaelic words have an initial **s** which doesn't always appear in their English cognates. In most cases this 'movable' **s** was there in the Indo-European root, and survives in some languages but not in others, and often alternates between them – English 'sneeze' is German *niesen*, for instance. Gaelic also has examples of the same word with and without the **s**, according to the dialect of the speaker. Other languages also do this; compare for instance English 'thrum' and 'strum'. So **sneachd** and snow are cognate, while the classical cognates 'nival, niveous' etc from Latin have lost the **s**. Other examples are:

sgeilb – Lochgilphead. **Sgeilb** (and the alternative form **gilb**) means 'chisel'; Loch Gilp in Argyll is supposed to be chisel-shaped. For the Gaelic **b** see §1. Classical cognates, with metathesis, are 'hieroglyph', the chiselled-out sacred writings of Ancient Egypt, 'glyptic' etc. Also cognate is *sculpture* etc, where the Latin, from which the English is borrowed, shows this moveable **s**.

slaic – lacerate. **Slaic** is 'a thump, blow'. There is also the related verb **slac** 'to beat, thrash'.

slat – lath. **Slat** is 'a rod, a stick'. A lath is a thin strip of wood used in plastering etc. A common compound is **slat-tomhais** 'yardstick'.

smachd – might, mechanics. **Smachd** means 'authority, discipline'. For the Gaelic **d** see §7.

smal – mole. **Smal** is 'a dark spot, stain', and mole is a spot on the skin. For the vowel change see §31; the Old English form was *mal*.

smug – mucus. **Smug** means 'snot, spittle', the latter more commonly in the form **smugaid**. Also related is **muc** 'pig' with its prominent snout, with an English cognate 'myxomatosis', a viral disease of the mucous membranes in rabbits. **Muc** appears in a number of placenames, but the best known, the Inner Hebridean island of Muck, refers to the whale, in Gaelic **muc-mhara** 'sea pig'.

snaidhm – node. **Snaidhm** is 'a knot' (also related), node being a classical cognate. For the vowel change see §31. A relationship with **snàth** 'thread', mentioned below, has also been suggested.

snàmh – natant. **Snàmh** means 'swim'. The village of Colintraive, **Caol an t-Snàimh** 'the Narrows of the Swimming' on the Kyles of Bute, commemorates the swimming of cattle to and from the island of Bute.

sneadh – nit. For the vowel change see §33 and for Gaelic **d** see §7. Also see §24 regarding English **h**.

snìomh – nematode. **Snìomh** means '(to) spin' (wool, to produce yarn), and a nematode is a thread-worm, a cause of disease in livestock. Also related are **snàth** 'thread' and **snàthad** 'needle', the latter appearing in Inversnaid, **Inbhir Snàthaid** 'Mouth of the Needle Burn', on the east bank of Loch Lomond. This may be a reference to its passage through a very narrow gorge, or an allusion to the 'foam flutes' mentioned by Gerard Manley Hopkins in his poem *Inversnaid*. For Gaelic **i** but English **e** see §36.

speach – bike. **Speach** is 'a wasp', and a bike its nest. The **p** was a **b** in earlier Gaelic. See also **beach** (§33).

srac – rape. **Srac** means '(to) tear, plunder'. Since the word is not borrowed the **p** will be missing in the Gaelic; for **c** in its place compare **seachd**/septet, §20.

sruth – rhythm. **Sruth** means 'a current, stream, anything flowing'. The idea is 'a regular movement', so not surprisingly the root, without the moveable **s**, features in several rivers, notably Rhine and Rhone (English 'running'). Other classical cognates are 'rheum, rheostat' etc. **Sruth** occurs in some placenames, as in the several instances of Struan (**An Sruthan** – Perthshire, Skye, North Uist), and possibly Anstruther in Fife.

Borrowings with this feature include:

sgudal – gut. **Sgudal** is 'fish-guts', and hence 'rubbish, trash'. A noun from **cut**, borrowed from English 'to gut' (fish). For the **d** in **sgudal** see §7.

smalan – <u>melan</u>choly. Borrowed from Scots *malancoly*.

smàrag – emerald. Borrowed from Latin (originally Greek) *smaragdus*. French, which also borrowed the word, replaced the initial **s** with **é**, as explained in the introduction. English took the word from French, so the initial **s** is missing in English too.

snèap – neep. Borrowed from English or Scots.

spann – band. **Spann** (initial **sb** is not a permitted Gaelic combination) means 'a hinge, clasp'. The form **bann** is more common, and both are borrowed from English. For the Gaelic **nn** against English **nd** see §19. There is a possibility that **spann** may be from Old English *spann* 'a clasp', but it is, or was, used in Uist to mean 'to bind, tie tightly'.

spìocach – pinch. **Spìocach** means 'miserly, niggardly' and pinch has the sense of 'stint, be sparing with'. This meaning of pinch is attested in the early 14th century, and was probably in use well before that, so this may be the source of the Gaelic. The etymology of pinch is a bit uncertain, but Gaelic regularly drops the letter **n** before **c** in Indo-European derivatives, as shown in §19, resulting in a long vowel as compensation, hence the accent in **spìocach**.

sporan – purse. As the **p** suggests, the Gaelic has been borrowed, from Latin. It is possible, however, that the initial **s** is due to metathesis (changing position of the **s** and **p**).

Moveable s

sprèidh – <u>pred</u>atory, de<u>pred</u>ation. **Sprèidh** means 'cattle', and the word is borrowed from Latin *praeda* 'booty', cattle raids being a feature of Highland life. Scots has *spreath*, *spreach*, *spreith*, 'cattle, plunder', borrowed from Gaelic.

stanna – tun. **Stanna** is 'a tub, barrel'. Borrowed from English. There is also a form **tunna.**

steàrnan – tern. Borrowed from Norse or English, since the **s** was there in Old English. The word was used as a nickname for people living at the Kyle of Lochalsh, presumably from the large amount of terns found there.

Sometimes, however, the initial **s** is missing in Gaelic but found in English cognates. Thus **pòs**, 'marry', mentioned above (§19), is cognate with English 'spouse'. Other instances are:

ceò – sky. **Ceò** means 'mist'. In Old English *scio* meant 'cloud'. A classical cognate is 'ob<u>scu</u>re', and possibly, if the word is related to **ciar** 'dark, dusky' – the next entry - also the various scia/scio-compounds, as 'sciophyte', a shade-loving plant. The general idea is 'covered up'. Skye is known as **Eilean a' Cheò**, 'the Isle of the Mist'. See also **ciar** below.

ciar – sciarid, and the various scia- compounds. **Ciar** means 'dusky, shady', and a sciarid is a dark-coloured fly. Skiagram and skiagraph are old-fashioned words for an x-ray. See also **ceò** above.

cra<u>i</u>ceann – skin. The earlier spelling of the latter part of the word as *cionn*, independently obsolete, makes the relationship with 'skin' clearer. Also found is **bo<u>i</u>ceann** or **boi<u>cionn</u>** 'goatskin', English cognate 'buckskin', and **uaini<u>c</u>eann** or **uaini<u>cionn</u>** 'lambskin'.

cuilean – Scylla. **Cuilean** means 'a puppy'. In classical mythology Scylla was a monster who devoured sailors passing through the Straits of Messina. She was portrayed by the Roman poet Vergil as wearing a girdle of dogs' heads round her waist, and ancient scholars thought that her name was derived from a Greek word for puppy (*skulax*). Modern scholars are not certain about this.

ealtainn – spalt. **Ealtainn** is 'a razor'. Spalt means 'to tear off, chip away'. The letter **p** is missing in the Gaelic, as mentioned in §20.

mial – small. **Mial** means 'a louse', but formerly meant 'an animal'. In Norse *smali* meant 'small sheep' or 'cattle'; 'any animal' according to Dwelly, now an obsolete meaning. Related also are 'molars', the teeth which grind food into small pieces.

mìog – smirk. **Mìog** means 'smile', and the form **smig** is also found. Classical cognates are 'mirror, miracle' etc, the idea being something amazing, wonderful.

mùch – smoke. **Mùch** means 'smother, extinguish', an activity which usually engenders a fair amount of smoke, and had the meaning 'smoke' in Early Irish, as does Welsh *mwg*. **Mùchan** was a smoke hole in the wall of a building, the precursor of a chimney, and **smùchan** was also used in Perthshire to mean 'smoke'. For the vowel change see §38.

tàmh – stamina. **Tàmh** is 'rest, quiet'. The idea of stamina is 'staying power'.

taois – stearic, steatite. **Taois** is 'dough'; stearic and steatite refer to fat and suet.

tarbh – steer. **Tarbh** means 'bull' and a steer is a young ox. Also related are Taurus, the zodiac sign of the Bull, and Minotaur. The word is common in placenames, as Tarfside, the village on the river Tarf in Glen Esk, Angus.

tàth – stand. **Tàth** means '(to) join together' – rabbet (rebate), glue, cement etc. The idea is 'to set in position'. The final **d** of 'stand' is not part of the Indo-European root; neither Greek nor Latin has it, nor, coincidentally, does Scots (*staun*, *stan*).

Moveable S

teach – <u>steg</u>osaur. **Teach** means 'house'. The modern form used is **taigh**[28] but **teach** occurs in **a-steach** 'into the house'. A stegosaur was a large lizard of the dinosaur era, covered in a kind of armour plating. The several steg- compounds in English indicate a covering. The idea of **teach** and **taigh** is 'a roof over your head'. Other cognates are 'thatch' (§28), 'tegula' (a roof tile), the botanical 'tegmen', and 'toga', the Roman all-covering garment, and 'tile' itself. For Gaelic **ea** as English **e** see §34.

tha – <u>sta</u>nd. **Tha** means 'am, is, are'. The idea of 'stand' is to 'continue to exist', and it is used as a verb to be in other languages, as Italian *come sta?* 'how are you?'. And as mentioned in the introduction regarding French 'rules', *étais* 'was' would have earlier begun *sta*…

thig – <u>sti</u>ch. **Thig** means 'come'. Stich is a line of poetry, but in earlier Greek, from which the word comes, it referred to a line or row of soldiers on the march. The idea is that of moving on foot. There is possibly also a connection with Scots *steg* and *staik* 'to stride with long steps or in a stately way', a sense also found in German *staken* 'to walk stiffly'.

---

[28] This is the form found in placenames, and there are many of these, as Tighnabruich, Tyndrum etc. It occurs even in England, as Tywardreath in Cornwall, an area which retained a Celtic language much later than any other part of that country. The two forms **a-steach** and **a-staigh**, like **a-mach** and **a-muigh** 'out(side)', reflect different cases of the old Gaelic noun, the forms without the letter **i** being the accusative (objective) case, indicating motion – into the house (as opposed to being in the house).

Borrowings are:

pleadh – splay(foot). Borrowed from English. The form **spleadh** is also found.

pòr – spore. **Pòr** means 'seed'. The basic sense is that of sowing, scattering, and as the **p** indicates, the word is borrowed, presumably from English, though it's of Greek origin; the Sporades are a group of Greek islands in the Aegean, so called because they are scattered (i.e. not in a group). Hence also English 'sporadic'.

§24 S AS ENGLISH H

An initial **s** in Gaelic is sometimes represented by an **h** in related English words. This dropping of **s** is also a well-known feature of languages as diverse as Greek and Welsh. So **sè** or **sia** 'six' is cognate with 'hexagon, hexameter' etc, and, of course, six itself. Related Gaelic placenames will naturally keep the **s** form, as Portinisherrich, **Port Innis Sia- Ràmhaich** 'Port of the Island of the Six-oared (boat)' on the east side of Loch Awe, Argyll (there was a ferry here crossing the loch). Other instances of this missing **s** in English are:

sàl – halogen. **Sàl** means 'salt', and halogen is a salt-inducing chemical; there are many other halo- compounds, generally of a scientific nature. Also cognate are 'salt' itself, 'saline' etc, and this is the form found in placenames such as Salen (Mull etc) indicating an inlet of the sea.

seachd – heptagon, heptameter etc. **Seachd** means 'seven' – which is also cognate. For the missing **p** in Gaelic see §20. Also cognate are forms with the **s**, as 'septet, September' etc.

seàrr – Harpy. **Seàrr** means '(to) scythe, cut with a sickle'. In Greek mythology Harpies were rapacious creatures, half-woman and half-bird who snatched away people and objects. For the missing **p** in Gaelic see §20.

sèid – hist. **Sèid** means '(to) blow' (of the wind). See also §8.

sneadh – nit. The old English form was *hnitu*. See also §23, and for the Gaelic **d** see §7.

soc – hog. **Soc** means 'a snout', particularly that of a pig and also, from its shape, 'a ploughshare' (English 'sock'). Also related is 'sow'. Succoth, **an Socach**, near Strachur, Argyll, may refer to pigs, or to the tapering piece of land between two converging streams. There are also many mountains with this name.

suain – <u>hypno</u>tise. **Suain** means 'deep sleep'. For the missing **p** in Gaelic see §20. Also cognate is '<u>somn</u>olent' and the various other somno- compounds.

§25 S AS ENGLISH H IN LOANS

There are a few Gaelic words beginning with **s** which are borrowed from English words beginning with the letter **h**. Since words in Gaelic don't start with **h** (see §16), such English words were treated as if they began with a vowel (just as they are pronounced by some speakers in England). So, take the word 'heckle', a comb for flax, hemp etc. This was taken as eckle, which then was liable to be treated according to Gaelic grammatical rules; in this case it might be regarded as beginning with **s**. Feminine nouns (and masculine ones in some cases) which begin with **s** don't sound the **s** when they are preceded by the definite article. So **an t-sùil** 'the eye' is pronounced something like *an too-il*. 'The heckle' then became *an t-seiceal*, where the **s** was silent. When the definite article is absent the **s** is sounded as normal; **sùil** is pronounced *soo-il*, and in the same way the form **seiceal** would have evolved. There is certainly something rather arbitrary about this; such words could well have ended up with an initial **t** in Gaelic – see §30 below. But we must remember that such words were borrowed by a largely illiterate population who simply adapted words to their existing speech patterns. Another factor to bear in mind is that with a lenited **s** (written **sh**) in Gaelic the **s** is not pronounced, so **sh** is sounded like English **h**. Other words with this feature are:

saidhe – hay. The **dh**, which is not pronounced, is there simply to separate the syllables.

sainnseal – handsel. A handsel is a gift to mark the New Year, or a new house, and so on. For the missing **d** see §19, though the Gaelic may reflect the Scots form *hansel*.

seabhag – hawk. Hawk was earlier *hafoc*. **Baile nan Seabhag** 'Hawks' Farm' is one of the names for Old Croggan in the south of Mull.

siùrsach – whore. The **w** is not pronounced, of course, particularly in the Scots form *hure* (various spellings), so the word would have sounded as if it began with **h**. The Gaelic pronunciation seems to have been influenced by the Scots form.

§26 SG as English SH

This combination has been mentioned in §13 above in connection with Gaelic **g** in place of English **c** (or **k**). It also represents English **sh** at the beginning of a word. Gaelic **sg** is pronounced **sk**, and this echoes a change found also in English; 'shirt' and 'skirt' are in origin the same word, as are 'ship' and 'skiff', and other instances appear below. So **sgàth** 'shadow, shade' is related to both these English words, as is another Gaelic word **sgàil**, of similar meaning. Classical cognates are the several scoto-compounds relating to shadow, darkness, as 'scotoma' (a blind spot in vision). For the change of vowel to **o** see §31. Other instances of this feature are:

sgadan – shad. **Sgadan** means 'herring', and shad is a fish related to herring, although it is also used to describe other kinds of fish. Cognate also is 'skate' (for the **d/t** interchange see §7), a fish of the ray family. Garscadden, **Gart Sgadain** 'Herring Yard' is an area of Glasgow.

sgar – shear. **Sgar** means 'cut, sever'. Scarista, **Sgarastadh**, in the south-west of Harris, is the village with a cut or depression in the landscape.

sgiamhach – shimmer. **Sgiamhach** means 'beautiful'.

sgil – shell. **Sgil** means '(to) husk, shell' (grain, peas etc). For the change of vowel see §36. Related also are 'scale', one of the thin plates or shells on reptiles, fish etc, and 'skull'.

sgòth – shade. **Sgòth** is 'a cloud', and is another form of **sgàth** mentioned at the beginning of this section.

sgraing – shrink. **Sgraing** is 'a scowl'. The idea is surliness, meanness of nature, reluctance, unwillingness.

sgreuch – shriek. Also cognate is 'screech'.

Borrowings include:

sgalag – mar<u>shal</u>. **Sgalag** is 'a servant', and marshal was originally a groom, a horse (mare) servant, and is now also a common surname. Borrowed from Norse. The same root appears in the now virtually obsolete *sene<u>schal</u>*, 'a steward, an old retainer', the first part of which is cognate with Gaelic **sean**, 'old'.

sgeilp – shelf. Probably borrowed from the Scots form *skelf*. *Skelf* is itself the northern form of shelf, as mentioned above.

sgillinn – shilling. **Sgillinn** means 'penny'. Borrowed from English. When Scotland and England had separate currencies the Scots penny was roughly equivalent in value to the English one at the time of Robert I (about 1300), but gradually lost value over the centuries. By the time of the accession of James VI to the joint throne of Scotland and England in 1603 it was worth one-twelfth of the value of an English penny, and remained so until the single-currency union in 1707.[29] Before the 17th century a penny was **peighinn** in Gaelic, borrowed from English, and this is the form found in various placenames, as Pennyghael, **Peighinn a' Ghàidheil** 'the Pennyland of the Gael' in Mull. The reference is to land rental value, like the several Penningtons in England, and the word is probably related to 'pawn', itself from Latin *pannus* meaning 'cloth, garment', clothing being a most frequently pawned article.

sgioba – ship. **Sgioba** is 'the crew of a ship'. Borrowed from Norse. For the Gaelic **b** see §1.

---

[29] Some younger readers may need reminding that in pre-decimal days there were twelve pennies in a shilling.

sgìre – shire. Borrowed from English. **Sgìre** now means 'a district, parish, county', the last being named after a count - not copied in Gaelic. A shire is now **siorrachd** or **siorramachd**, from English 'sheriff', from which Gaelic **siorram** is borrowed; the idea is 'a division (of territory), a cutting', from English 'shear' (see also under **sgar** above. **Sliabh an t-Siorraim**, Sheriffmuir in Perthshire, was the scene of an indecisive battle during the 1715 Jacobite uprising.

§27 SR AS ENGLISH STR

This letter is missing in certain Gaelic words where the combination **sr** becomes **str** in related words in English. It should be pointed out, however, that many Gaelic speakers pronounce initial **sr-** as **str-**. So **srath** 'valley' is English 'strath', which is, of course, borrowed from Gaelic. Other examples of this feature are:

srad – star, a<u>ster</u>isk, a<u>ster</u>oid, a<u>stro</u>naut, a<u>stro</u>nomy. **Srad** is 'a spark' (from the fire), a sparkling. More common is the diminutive **sradag**. Another classical cognate is 'stellar', the Latin form of which was earlier *sterula*.

sreang – string.

sruth – stream. **Sruth** means 'a current, flow'. Another cognate is 'rheum', a flow or discharge from the nose, lungs etc. For its missing initial **s** see §23. Related also is the Norse placename root *strome*, with several instances in the north and west of the country, as Stroma 'Current Island' in the Pentland Firth and Stromness in Orkney. See also **sream** below.

Borrowings include:

sràbh – straw. Borrowed from English.

sream – stream. **Sream** means 'rheum', and is thought to be a borrowing from English 'stream'. It could, however, be based on 'rheum', with an additional initial **s**, as discussed in §23.

sringlean – strangles. Borrowed from English. Strangles, also known as vives and equine distemper, is a bacterial disease in horses. It is also known in Gaelic as **galar-greigh**.

srùb – stroup. **Srùb** means 'a spout' (of a kettle etc), and this is the sense of *stroup* in Scots. For the **b** in Gaelic see §1. Borrowed from Scots. **Srùb** is also a verb, '(to) spout', and can also mean a cockle, a common type of shellfish. Ardnastruban, **Àird nan Srùban** 'Promontory of the Cockles' is in Grimsay, North Uist. The **t** in the English version of the name reflects the fact that initial **sr** is not an English combination.

This feature can also occur within a word, as **eisir/oisir** – oyster.

§28 T as English TH

Gaelic **t** represents English **th**, particularly at the start of a word. This is a feature of words borrowed from English as **taing** 'thank'; for the Gaelic **g** see §13. Since all Gaelic speakers are now bilingual and can pronounce **th** as in English, a change to a single **t** might be thought to be no longer necessary, but it reflects traditional sounds of the language; **th** of English is not a Gaelic sound.[30] Other borrowed examples are:

brot – broth. The English form would be quite acceptable in Gaelic – such a word exists, meaning 'a scab, a rash' (on the skin) and 'a halo' (round the moon) but would be pronounced *bro*.

matamataig – mathematic. From English.

miotas – myth. From English.

steatasgop – stethoscope. From English.

tùis – thus, thurible. **Tùis** is 'incense'; thus is another word for frankincense and a thurible is a censer. Borrowed from Latin. Also related is the plant thyme, which has been burnt from ancient times for its sweet smell or for fumigation purposes. This derivation is not a factor in any of its various Gaelic forms, of which the commonest is **lus an rìgh** 'the king's herb'; a fuller version of this appears in the magnificent, if rather impractical, **lus mhic rìgh Bhreatainn beag nam bruach** 'little plant of the son of the king of Britain of the banks' mentioned by the Rev Fr Allan McDonald in his collection of Gaelic words from South Uist and Eriskay.

Words of Gaelic origin with this feature are:

tana – thin. Also related is 'tenuous'. **Tana** also means 'shallow', and the Tan is a shallow stretch of water between the

---

[30] Although the pronunciation of **r** with a slender vowel in some areas comes close to it.

Cumbrae Islands off Largs. Related also is La Tène (the Shallows), familiar as the name of a Celtic Iron Age civilisation of the edge of Lake Neuchatel in Switzerland.

tàrr – thairm. Both words mean 'belly, guts'. The Scots form *thairm* is familiar from its mention in the first verse of Burns' *Address to a Haggis*.

tart – thirst. Classical cognates are 'torrid, terrain' and the various terra- compounds (terracotta etc), the idea being <u>dry</u> land. The same Gaelic root appears in Glen Turret, **Gleann Turraid** 'the Dry Glen', north of Crieff in Perthshire and again off Glen Roy north of Spean Bridge. See also **tìr** §36.

teach – thatch. **Teach** means 'house'; see under **teach** §23. See also **tughadh** below.

tiugh – thick. For the Gaelic **g** see §13.

tlàth – thole, <u>tela</u>mon. **Tlàth** means 'mild, gentle, mellow'. Of a person the idea is easy-going, prepared to put up with something. Thole (with metathesis) means 'to put up with' and telamon is a more literal extension of this. A telamon is a stone figure of a man used as a pillar to support a building. It was common in Greek and Roman temples etc and is the male equivalent of a female caryatid similarly used, e.g. on the Acropolis at Athens. For the Gaelic **à** but English **o** see §31.

toil – thole. **Toil** means 'inclination, desire'. The idea is something one is prepared to accept. A classical cognate is 'tolerate', with the sense 'to bear up'.

<u>torrannach</u> – Thor, thorium. **Torrannach** means 'thunderous', Thor is the old Norse god of Thunder, and thorium is a metal named for its importance in nuclear power. Related also are the Gaelic Thor forenames, **Torcal(l)** (Torquil) and **Tormod** (Norman), and some surnames, as Thorburn. There are many placenames in the north-west and in England named by settlers

from Scandinavia based on Norse personal names derived from Thor. Glen Tanar, however, near Aboyne, Aberdeenshire, is named after the thundering river which courses through it; for the metathesis see §40.

tre – through, thrill. **Tre** means 'through' and thrill (related to 'drill') originally meant 'to pierce, make a hole in', a meaning found in 'nostril' (nose hole). Drill and thrill show the Germanic **d/th** interchange mentioned in the introduction.

treabh – thorp(e), turbulent, trabeate, Trevor. **Treabh** means '(to) plough' but it earlier had the related meaning of farm building, house, and hence a cultivated area, farming community, a sense still found in **treabhair**(**e**). Thorp(e) is 'a village' (now found mainly in placenames in England and as a surname), while turbulent refers to a lot or crowd of people, and trabeate refers to horizontal beams, though the Latin word from which it comes was sometimes used to mean 'a roof'. This also accounts for the modern Gaelic **aitreabh** 'a building'. The overall sense of farming community buildings occurs in several placenames, as Ochiltree 'High Settlement' in Ayrshire and elsewhere, where the suffix is from the cognate Welsh/Old British *tref*, which is also the origin of the placename and personal name Trevor.

trì – three.

trod – threat. **Trod** means 'a scolding, reprimand'. For the Gaelic **d** see §7. Cognate also is 'intrude'. See also **truaill** next.

truaill – thrust. **Truaill** means 'a sheath'. Again, 'intrude' is a cognate, the idea with this, and **trod** previously, being that of pushing in, interrupting.

tughadh – thatch. See **teach** above. **Taigh-tughaidh** is 'a black house', the traditional Highlands and Islands thatched dwelling, preserved as a museum in various locations.

tulach – thumb. **Tulach** is a hillock. The general idea is a lump, swelling (the thumb being the widest of the fingers). Also cognate are tuber, tumour, tumulus and the medical term tylosis (an inflammation).

In all the above **th** in English cognates is unvoiced (like **th** in thin). An example with voiced **th** (as in then) is 'thou', related to Gaelic **tu**[31] 'you' (singular). The related English word 'thy' is a rare instance of the same word sound but with unvoiced **th** (thigh) having a totally different meaning, something English generally avoids with initial **th.**

---

[31] A less common, but in certain circumstances obligatory, form of **thu**.

§29 T AS ENGLISH H

A Gaelic word sometimes starts with a **t** where the related English word begins with **h** or a vowel. This is because, as explained in §25, **h** doesn't normally begin a Gaelic word, and so such English words were regarded as beginning with a vowel. Gaelic masculine nouns which start with a vowel retain a **t** when the definite article stands before them; so **eilean** 'island', but **an t-eilean** 'the island'.[32] So 'the hall' when borrowed became *an t-alla*, confused by a largely illiterate population with **an talla**, hence the form **talla** 'hall' today. See also **ceall** §2. Similar misunderstandings have occurred in English; 'adder' (snake) was originally *nadder* (hence the Gaelic cognate **nathair**), and similar confusion lies behind the words *apron*, *orange*, *umpire*, *newt* and *nickname*. See also **uimhir**, §42.

Other instances of this feature in Gaelic are:

tabh – haaf. **Tabh** means 'sea, ocean', and *haaf* is a Norse word used in the Northern Isles to describe fishing grounds at sea.

tadhal – hail. **Tadhal** means 'a goal', originally in shinty but now also in football, and a hail is the name for a goal in the annual hand ba game in Jedburgh. The sense is thought to represent the reaction of the scorer, his team, and/or the crowd. Again the **dh** is not really a part of the word but is there just to separate the syllables. Borrowed from English.

taigeis – haggis. Borrowed from Scots.

talan – hallan. **Talan** means 'a partition, an internal wall', and *hallan(d)* is a Scots word of similar meaning, from which the Gaelic seems borrowed.

---

[32] This is what lies behind the less common alternative forms **Tearach** and **Tiortach** for the more usual **Hearach** and **Hiortach**, natives of Harris and St Kilda respectively.

tiota – iota. **Tiota** means 'an instant'. The idea is a very small period of time, a jot, borrowed by English from the smallest letter in the Greek alphabet.

todha – hoe. Borrowed from English.

togsaid – hogshead. A hogshead is a large cask holding various amounts of wine etc. Borrowed from English.

tolm – holm. **Tolm** is 'a hillock', its meaning in Old English, though holm now means 'an island in a river'. German *Holm* has both these meanings. The Gaelic form occurs in Tolmachan, **An Tolmachan** 'the Small Hillock', about six miles west of Tarbert, Harris, and **Tolm**, Holm near Stornoway, Lewis overlooking the rocks (**Biastan Thuilm**) which caused the sinking of the troopship *Iolaire* on New Year's Day 1919, with much loss of life.

The reverse of the above process is found in **umpaidh**, probably from Scots *tump(h)ie* (various spellings). Both words mean a slow-witted, stupid person, and Gaelic speakers could easily have heard *tumpie* with the definite article in Gaelic as **an t-umpaidh** instead of **an tumpaidh**, giving rise to the form **umpaidh** without the article. The letter **p** indicates that Gaelic was the borrower (see §20) and *tumpie* first appears in the 18th century in written form, and presumably even earlier orally.

§30 LOSS OF ENGLISH V

This is not a Gaelic letter, though it is a Gaelic sound represented by the letters **bh** and **mh**. Often, however, **bh** and **mh** are silent in the middle or at the end of a word. But the **v** sound has never been written in words like **dia** 'god', although it's there in cognates like 'diva, divine' etc. Other instances of this feature include:

aois – medi(a)eval. **Aois** means 'age'. The **v** appears also in the cognate 'ever', but not in 'age' and 'aye', which are also related; for the **g/y** interchange of the last two see §12.

beò – vivacious, revive, vivid. **Beò** means '(a)live'. The opening **b** would change to a **v** sound under certain grammatical circumstances, but there is, of course, no **v** sound in the middle of the Gaelic word as there is in the related words. There is also no internal **v** in the related viand(s) – i.e. a necessity of life – because the word has been borrowed from French, a language which routinely drops internal consonants which were there in earlier Latin. **Beò** illustrates another linguistic feature: some Gaelic words of Indo-European origin which begin with **b** are related to English equivalents which begin with **c** or **qu**. So **beò** is cognate with 'quick' (in its original meaning of alive, lively). Other words with this feature are **bò** and its cognate 'cow', **bean** (woman) and 'queen' (and the North-East *quine*), and **brà** and 'quern'. This last word appears in Auchenbrain, **Achadh na Bràthann** 'Field of the Quern', the name of a couple of farms (North and South) a few miles north of Mauchline, Ayrshire.

bò – bovine. **Bò** means 'a cow'. Also related are 'beef, buffalo, bugle, butter, bugloss'. See also under **beò** above

ciùin – civil. **Ciùin** means 'calm, easy-going, gentle', used of people, like civil in its sense of polite.

clò – clove, <u>clav</u>ier. **Clò** means (or meant – it's now obsolescent) 'a nail, peg, pin'. A clove, the dried flower bud used as a spice, is so called from its resemblance to a small nail. A clavier is the keyboard of an instrument such as the piano, whose sound was made using, amongst other things, a system of levers and pins. Other obscure musical instruments with the same root are clave, clavecin, clavicembalo, and clavichord.

còs – cave, cavity. Gartcosh, a few miles to the north-east of Glasgow, is thought to refer to a field with a cave in it.

grothlach – <u>grav</u>el. The English **v** suggests that it was borrowed from Old French (modern French *grève*, 'a beach').

leòr – Laverna. **Leòr** means 'plenty', and Laverna was the Roman patron goddess of gain (especially illegal). See also **luach** 'value' §39.

lì – <u>liv</u>id. **Lì** means 'colour' (usually of the face) and livid refers to a leaden, blueish complexion, black and blue.

nuadh – <u>nov</u>el. **Nuadh** means 'new, fresh'. See also §39. Glen Noe, a few miles north of Dalmally, 'the Fresh Green Glen', reflects an alternative form **nodha**.

othaisg – <u>ov</u>ine. **Othaisg** (sometimes spelt **òisg**) means 'a year-old ewe' ('ewe' also being cognate), and ovine refers to sheep in general.

sneachd – snow, <u>niv</u>al. **Sneachd** means 'snow', and 'nival' refers to plants etc growing in or under snow. Another Gaelic cognate **snighe** 'raindrops through a roof' has the **i** of nival. For the Gaelic initial **s** see §23.

There are also a couple of borrowings:

luidhear – louver, louvre. **Luidhear** is 'a vent, a chimney, funnel'. Borrowed from English, which took it from French, with its presumed meaning 'the opening' (*l'ouvert*). The Gaelic **dh** is again silent and there only to separate the syllables, which suggests that the **v** was not sounded in English at the time the word was borrowed.

pàillean – pa<u>v</u>ilion. **Pàillean** is 'a tent'. Borrowed from Scots *pallion* (various spellings), a form of 'pavilion'. The original meaning is 'butterfly', reflecting the fact that a tent was spread like a butterfly's wings.

Slightly different is **clobha** – clove(n). **Clobha** means 'tongs'. Although the **bh** is written here in this borrowing from Norse it is not pronounced as a **v** sound. The reference is to the split or forked shape of the implement.

The next sections, §31 to §39, again in alphabetical order according to the letters under discussion, deal with vowels.

Vowel changes are a feature of Gaelic nouns, and some of the differences between Gaelic words and their English cognates listed below are regularly found within Gaelic nouns themselves. Some examples are:

clach 'stone' with a genitive (possessive) case **cloiche**; so Clachnacuddin, **Clach na Cùdainn** 'the Stone of the Washing Tub' in Inverness, but Achnacloich, **Achadh na Cloiche** 'the Field of the Stone' near Oban.

allt 'burn, stream' with a genitive **uillt**; so Aultbea, **An t-Allt Beithe** 'the Birch Stream' on Loch Ewe in Ross & Cromarty, but Taynuilt, **Taigh an Uillt** 'the House by the Burn' near Oban.

creag 'rock' with a genitive **creige**; so Craignure, **Creag an Iubhair**[33] 'the Rock of the Yew Tree', but Craighouse, **Taigh na Creige** on Jura.

port 'port, harbour' with a genitive **puirt**; so Portnahaven, **Port na h-Abhainne** 'Port by the River' in Islay, but Tighphuirt, **Taigh a' Phuirt** 'House by the Port' by Glencoe village.

---

[33] There are other place names from iubhar in this country but the best known is in England from an Old British form of the word; York was earlier *Eboracum* 'Yew Tree Estate'.

§31 A AS ENGLISH O

Gaelic **a** or **à** often appears as **o** in related English words. This is an occasional feature of Gaelic, as **facal/focal** 'word', versions with **o** having an Irish flavour. It is, of course, a well-known feature of Scots, as tap (top), wrang (wrong) and so on. It can also occur within the same word in Gaelic, as mentioned above: **coise** is the genitive of **cas** 'foot, leg'. So **cas** is related to English 'coxa' (hip). Other instances are:

aisean – ossein, ossify. **Aisean** means 'a rib' and ossein is bone matter. An Indo-European **o** can become an **a** in Gaelic (and Sanskrit), as this section indicates. Related also are the various osteo- compounds, coined from Greek.

alt – fold (i.e. bend). **Alt** means 'a joint'. For the English initial **f** see §20.

a-màireach – to<u>morrow</u>.

amar – <u>ombro</u>meter, and other ombr- compounds. **Amar** is 'a trough, ditch, channel' (for rainwater) and an ombrometer is a rain gauge. Another classical cognate is <u>imbr</u>icate, 'with overlapping slates, tiles' (to exclude rain). For the missing **b** in **amar** see **imleag** §13. **Amar-snà(i)mh** is in common use for a swimming pool.

amh – <u>omo</u>phagy. **Amh** means 'raw', and omophagy is the eating of raw food, especially meat.

amhach – <u>om</u>oplate. **Amhach** is 'neck', and omoplate is a medical term for the shoulder blade.

a-mhàin – <u>mono</u>cle. **A-mhàin** means 'only, alone'. There are dozens of mono- compounds (from Greek) with this meaning in English.

bàbhan – <u>bo</u>vine. **Bàbhan** is 'a cattle fold', and appears in English as 'bawn'.

cairt – cortex. **Cairt** is 'bark' (of a tree) and cortex is the outer layer of bark.

cast – ho(a)st. Both words mean 'a cough'. See §2 and §7.

damh – <u>dom</u>estic. **Damh** means 'ox' or 'stag'. The idea is that of the ox as a domesticated animal, as indeed deer would be in Lapland.

dàn – <u>don</u>ate. **Dàn** means 'destiny'; the sense is 'what is given (by fate)'. Also cognate is *da(t)scha,*, a house in the Russian countryside on land given as a gift by the Czar.

dea<u>mhais</u> – mow, mead(ow), after<u>math</u>. **Deamhais** is 'shears'. The general idea is 'cutting'. The dea- prefix means 'two' – a reference to the blades of the shears – like English di- in dimeter, a verse of two feet. Related is the surname Mather 'Mower'.

drannd(an) – drone. **Drannd(an)** means 'a hum, murmur', like the noise made by bees, the male of which is of course called a drone. A possible classical cognate is '<u>thren</u>ody' a mournful ode, with typical English **t** where Gaelic **d** – see §7.

facal – vocal. **Facal**, mentioned at the beginning of this section, means 'word'.

falt – wool. **Falt** means 'hair'. Wool now has a **u** sound, but note German *Wolle*. See also §9.

garg – Gorgon. **Garg** means 'ferocious' and a Gorgon was a fabulous Greek monster, fierce and petrifying.

gnàth – know. **Gnàth** means 'custom, habit'. See §13.

làr – floor. See §20 where English **f** corresponds to missing Gaelic **p.**

GAELIC AND ENGLISH

mair – <u>mora</u>torium. **Mair** means '(to) last, endure'.

manadh – (ad)monition. **Manadh** means 'omen'.

marbh – morbid. **Marbh** means 'dead'. Also cognate, with different vowels, are 'check<u>mate</u>', '<u>mat</u>ador', 'murder', and 'murrain' (a disease, usually fatal, in cattle). **Marbh** occurs in Blairnamarrow, **Blàr nam Marbh** 'Field of the Dead', about three miles south of Tomintoul.

màthair – mother.

sgàth – scotoma. **Sgàth** means 'shade, cover'. See §26.

snàth – snood. **Snàth** means 'a thread', and a snood is a band of wool, string etc once commonly used to bind up a girl's hair. The English has a **u** vowel sound, but was earlier *snod*; its etymology is obscure.

tàladh – dole. **Tàladh** is an act of 'enticing, alluring', and dole is a Scots legal term for criminal intent. The idea is that of guile.

tuarastal – toll, talent. **Tuarastal** means 'salary, wages'. Toll is money paid to use bridges, roads etc, and talent was an old Greek unit of money, often mentioned in the Bible. The modern meaning of talent as ability arose later from its mention in the parable of the talents in St. Matthew's gospel. An alternative explanation takes the ending from the now obsolete **dàil**, a portion (of land and its people), the origin of <u>Dal</u>riada.

Borrowings with this feature include:

aifreann – offering. **Aifreann** means 'a mass' in the Roman Catholic Church. The word appears in Inchaffray (Abbey), **Innis Aifrinn** 'Meadow of the Mass', a few miles east of Crieff, Perthshire. Borrowed from Latin.

àmhainn – oven. Borrowed from English.

A AS ENGLISH O

càl – cole. Cole is a general word for the cabbage and kail family, and **càl** also describes these plants. Borrowed from Latin. Also cognate is 'cauliflower'.

cnap – knob. **Cnap** means 'a lump'. Borrowed from Norse. The word also means 'a hillock', and is found in several placenames; Knapdale 'Hillock Dale' at the north end of Kintyre is probably the best known.

langasaid – long (seat). **Langasaid** is 'a long bench, settee' etc and is borrowed from Scots *langsettle* (various forms). The root *lang*, borrowed from Norse, occurs in various places in the Hebrides, as Loch Langavat (Long Water) in Lewis.

mag – mock. Borrowed from English. For the Gaelic **g** see §13.

manach – monk. Borrowed from Latin. The word occurs in several placenames, as Balivanich, **Baile a' Mhanaich** 'the Monk's Farmstead' in Benbecula. **A' Mhanachainn** 'the Monastery' is the Gaelic name for Beauly. The **o** vowel in English reflects the meaning of monk, which is 'solitary, alone' (mono-), as indicated under **a-mhàin** above.

rathad – road. Borrowed from English.

spàl – spool. **Spàl** means 'a shuttle'. Borrowed from Norse. Again, the English now has a **u** sound, but the Norse was *spola*.

stràc – stroke. Borrowed from Scots. The word is now used for the slash symbol of internet addresses and for an accent over a vowel (as in **stràc**).

trang – throng. **Trang** means 'busy'. Borrowed from Scots. For the Gaelic **t** but English **th** see §28; Scots also has the form *trang*, however.

§32 AO AS VARIOUS ENGLISH VOWELS

This sound, a bit like French *oeu* or German *ö*, corresponds to a variety of vowels in English cognates. English **a** appears in:

aodann – ante. **Aodann** means 'face'. The idea is 'facing, in front of, before'. See §7.

faodhail – wade. **Faodhail** is 'a ford' (between islands). Also **fadhail**. See §9.

glaodh – clay. **Glaodh** means 'glue', which is another cognate. See §13.

laoch – lay, laic. **Laoch** is 'hero, champion', earlier 'a soldier'. The general idea is a non-clerical person. In Greek, from which the English is derived (via Latin), the word originally meant simply people, and was commonly found in personal names, as Laomedon 'people ruler', a king of Troy.

staoin – stannary. **Staoin** is 'tin'; a stannary is a tin-mining area, and the Stannaries was the name given to the tin mining regions of Devon and Cornwall.

English **ae** appears in **caoch** – caecilian, caecus, cecity. **Caoch** means 'blind'. Caecilian is a reptile like an earthworm with defective eyesight, and caecus is a medical term for a blind sac. Related also is the female name **Sìle(as)**, a Gaelic version of Cecily which itself is, via Anglo-French, ultimately from the Roman family name Caecilius, 'blind'. The more usual word for blind is **dall**, for which see §42.

English **e** appears in:

claon – lean. **Claon** means 'inclined, oblique, sloping'. For the Gaelic **c** see §2.

AO AS VARIOUS ENGLISH VOWELS

saoghal – secular. **Saoghal** means 'world'. The idea is 'worldly, of this world' (not the next).

English **i** appears in:

caoin – whine. **Caoin** means '(to) weep'. For the Gaelic **c** see §2.

fraoch – erica. See also §10.

maoth – <u>mit</u>igate. **Maoth** means 'soft, delicate'. This is thought to be the meaning of Muthil, **Maothail** in Fife, with a reference to the gentle terrain. Related also is **meath** 'fade, decay'.

naodh – nine. Another form is **naoi**, and this perhaps what is found in Kilninian, one explanation of which is **Cill Naoi Nighean** 'Church of the Nine Maidens', on Mull. (Another explanation refers to St Ninian.)

slaod – slide. **Slaod** means '(to) drag'. Both languages retain their own vowel in Sliddery, **Slaodraidh**, a village and river on the south coast of Arran, with some historical reference to dragging. There is also Sliddery Point on the west side of Wigtown bay.

English **o** appears in:

caomh – homely. **Caomh** means 'gentle'. See §2.

maorach – moray. **Maorach** means 'shellfish' and moray is a type of eel. The word is thought to occur in Arivirig, **Àirigh Mhaoraich** 'Shellfish Shieling', a settlement on the east coast of the island of Coll.

plaosg – phloem. **Plaosg** means 'a husk, shell, peel' and phloem is plant tissue. The **p** suggests that the Gaelic has been borrowed, but it is not clear from where. There is, however, an earlier alternative form **blaosg**.

saothair – sore. **Saothair** means 'work, labour'. The idea is that of hard labour, pain.

English **u** appears in:

aon – unit, unite etc. **Aon** means 'one'. In placenames it takes the form **aonach**, with the meanings 'unite' (gatherings, markets etc), and 'single, solitary' (remote hills, moors etc); the former appears in **Drochaid an Aonachain**, Spean Bridge, about ten miles north of Fort William.

draoidh – druid. The English is borrowed, and reflects another Gaelic spelling **druidh** (also spelt with a **u** in Old Irish). A classical cognate may be 'dryad' (a wood nymph) if the suggestion that **draoidh** is related to the root *dru* meaning 'oak tree' is correct. Port an Righ, an area near Nigg, Ross & Cromarty is thought to be **Port an Draoidh** 'Port of the Druid', though there are other possibilities.

faoileag – gull. Both probably from Welsh *gwylan*. English has several initial **g/w** alternatives of the same meaning, as guard/ward, guerrilla/war, guile/wile etc, and initial **gw** in Welsh represents Gaelic **f** as *gwin*/**fion**, 'wine'.

glaodh – glue. Another cognate is 'clay': see above in this section.

maoin – munificence. **Maoin** means 'wealth, funds'. A common compound is **dìomhain** 'idle', where di- (English dis-) is a negative prefix. The idea is 'unwaged'.

saoil – soul. **Saoil** means 'think'. There is thought to be a mutual connection with a word meaning 'power, strength' in Church Slavonic.

English **y** used as a vowel appears in **caol** – kyle. **Caol** means 'narrow', often used of a narrow stretch of water, as in the numerous Kyles on the west coast. In placenames, however, other vowels are also used, including **ao** itself - Caol (Fort William),

AO AS VARIOUS ENGLISH VOWELS

Colintraive (Cowal), Kelman Hill (Aberdeenshire), Eddrachillis (Sutherland) and Ballachulish (Loch Leven).

Gaelic **ao** in borrowings include:

aoine – jejune. **Aoine** is 'a fast(ing), abstinence from food'. The word is now used only in the names of the days Wednesday, Thursday and Friday which, in Gaelic, relate to fast days. Jejune means empty, undernourished, but in Latin, from which it and **aoine** are borrowed, it referred to a fast day. The **j** would have had a **y** sound in Latin.

maor – mayor. **Maor** means 'a steward, an officer of the crown'. Borrowed from Latin. The word occurs in placenames such as the Mearns (i.e. Kincardineshire), of land historically administered by a crown officer.

snaoisean – sneeze. **Snaoisean** is 'snuff', the old name for which was sneezing powder. Borrowed from English.

taoitear – tutor. Borrowed from Latin or English.

§33 EA AS ENGLISH I

This combination frequently corresponds to **i** in related English words. There is often an **i** in the Gaelic word too, but in a different case. The spelling rules of modern Gaelic also have to be taken into account. So **fear** 'man' is cognate with 'v<u>i</u>rile'. For the **f/v** interchange see §9. Other examples of this feature are:

anam – animate. **Anam** means 'soul'. The general sense is 'breath, wind, spirit', and other cognates are <u>anemo</u>meter, anemone, animal, animus etc. **Anam** was *anim* in Old Irish, which would be nearer to its English cognates, but this spelling is not allowed in modern Gaelic. A related Gaelic word is **anail** 'breath'.

beach – bike. **Beach** is 'a bee', and a bike is a nest of wild bees or wasps. Contrast **sgeap** §13.

beatha – vital. **Beatha** means 'life'. **B** has a **v** sound in Gaelic when lenited according to certain rules of grammar.

ceann – Kin (in placenames). **Ceann** means 'head', and the very common Kin- (as Kinlochleven, 'The Head of Loch Leven') is from a different case of **ceann**. This form is found also in **eanchainn** 'brain' i.e. in the head. The form Ken- is also found in placenames and in the surname Kennedy. See also §5.

eadar – inter. **Eadar** means 'between', and is quite common in placenames, usually keeping the Gaelic **d** as Eddrachillis in Sutherland; an exception is Etteridge just south of Newtonmore in Inverness-shire. As mentioned in §7, the difference is superficial; not only is the **d** in **eadar** sounded as **t**, it was written with a **t** (*eter*, *etar* etc) in Old Irish. But the English pronunciation of Eddrachillis and similar **eadar** words sounds the **d** like an English **d**, whereas in Gaelic **Eadar Dhà Chaolas** retains the **t** sound.

feachd – <u>vict</u>or. **Feachd** means 'army'. For the Gaelic **chd** see §6.

feall – wile. **Feall** means 'deceit, treachery'. See also §9.

greadan – grind, grist. **Greadan** is 'corn dried by roasting'.

meadhan – mid. Other cognates are 'medium, mean, med<u>i</u>aeval' etc.

mean – minor, minus, minute, menu. **Mean** (also **meanbh**) means 'small'. **A' Bheinn Mheanbh,** Ben Venue, just south of Loch Katrine in the Trossachs, is 'the Small Mountain'.

meanmna – mind. **Meanmna** means 'energy, spiritedness'. Also found is the form **mac-meanmna**, meaning 'imagination'.

measg – <u>misc</u>ellany, mix. **Measgaich** 'mix, mingle' is now the more common form of the verb. For the Gaelic **g** see §13.

nead – nide. **Nead** means 'nest', and nide (also called nye) is a brood or nest of pheasants. See also §8.

reachd – right. **Reachd** means 'a law, statute'. Classical cognates are '<u>reg</u>ulation, <u>rec</u>tor, <u>reg</u>al' etc.

seasg – de<u>sicc</u>ate. **Seasg** means 'dry, barren'. For the Gaelic **g** see §13.

sneadh – nit. For the initial **s** see §23.

sreang – string. For the missing **t** in Gaelic see §27.

teanga – linguist, tongue. **Teanga** means 'tongue'. The two English words well illustrate the richness of the language with its native and borrowed words. **Teanga** and its cognate tongue go back to Indo-European roots, but linguist was borrowed from Latin in the 16th century. The Latin word was originally *dingua* (so 'tongue' – for d/t interchange see §7), later *lingua*. This interchange between **d** and **l** was a feature of the classical languages, the best known example being U<u>l</u>ysses and O<u>d</u>ysseus, one and the same person.

Teanga is occasionally found in placenames, as Tong (Lewis), Teangue (Skye), Tongue (Sutherland).

treas – third, thrice. **Treas** means 'third'.

Borrowings with this feature include:

fea<u>lls</u>anach – <u>philos</u>opher. Borrowed from Latin.

feart – virtue. **Feart** means 'an attribute, quality'. Borrowed from Latin. For the Gaelic **f** see §9.

leabhar – <u>libr</u>ary. **Leabhar** means 'book'. Borrowed from Latin. The word appears in Pitliver 'Piece of Land of the Book' near Dunfermline, Fife; the book is the Bible, so it refers to church land in some way. Dunfermline was an important religious centre from the 10th century or earlier, with an abbey dating to the 12th century, and Pitliver estate is about two miles from the abbey.

seac – de<u>sicc</u>ated. **Seac** means '(to) wither'. Borrowed from Latin.

spealt – spill. **Spealt** is 'a splinter' and a spill is a thin strip of wood used to light a fire etc. Borrowed from Norse or Old English. A more common form is **spealg**, borrowed from Scots *spelk*.

steall – in<u>still</u>, di<u>still</u>. **Steall** means 'spout forth, squirt'. Steall is a well-known waterfall in Glen Nevis. The Gaelic form with the dark or back **l** is an exception to the 'rule' mentioned in §17. Also related is **stail** 'a still'; **taigh-staile** is a distillery. Borrowed from English.

§34 EA AS ENGLISH E

This combination also appears as **e** in related English words. The main reason for this is that Gaelic very rarely has the letter **e** by itself inside a word without another vowel along with it. So Gaelic has the form **each** 'horse', whereas English has the cognate 'equine'. This is the source of the surname MacEachern (various spellings) from the Kintyre tribe known to the Romans as Epidii; both names providing a good example of the p/q interchange mentioned in §5. Again, this is a convention of modern Gaelic spelling; Old Irish and other Celtic languages have the word with a simple **e**. The spelling rule (see introduction) also accounts for most instances. Other Gaelic examples are:

ceart – certain. **Ceart** means 'right, correct'.

deagh – decent. **Deagh** means 'good'. For the Gaelic **g** see §13.

deas – dexter(ity). **Deas** means 'right (hand), south'. For the Gaelic **s** see §22.

dìreach – direct. **Dìreach** means 'straight', and, as an adverb, 'exactly'.

feasgar – vesper. **Feasgar** means 'afternoon, evening'. For the Gaelic **f** see §9 and for the English **p** see §20.

geal – yellow. **Geal** means 'white'. The idea is 'bright, shining', as in **gealach** 'moon'. For the Gaelic **g** see §12.

leac – cromlech. **Leac** is 'a stone slab', and a cromlech is a prehistoric stone circle and also, formerly, a dolmen. Cromlech appears in Cromlix (an English plural, as happens occasionally with Gaelic placenames) a few miles north of Dunblane, Perthshire and **leac** itself is quite common, e.g. The Lecht, the ski resort near Tomintoul. Also the surname Auchinleck (Affleck). See also §20.

meadhan – medium.

meanmna – <u>men</u>tal. **Meanmna** means 'energy, spiritedness'.

nead – nest. See also §8, §33.

nèamh – <u>nemo</u>ral, <u>nemo</u>phila. **Nèamh** is 'heaven', and nemoral refers to a wooded pasture, grove, with nemophila being a genus of flowers which like such places. The idea is that of Paradise, which originally referred to a pleasure park or enclosed garden in Persia.

neart – Nero. **Neart** means 'strength'. The name of the Roman emperor Nero comes from a Sabine word meaning 'strong, brave'. Sabine is an old Italian dialect of the Oscan-Umbrian group, related to Latin, and so, like Gaelic, Indo-European. For another Roman emperor see §2 under **call**. A common compound is **fòirneart** 'violence'.

reachd – regulate. **Reachd** means 'a law, statute'. See also §33.

seach – <u>seq</u>uence, <u>sec</u>ond (i.e. following after), (en)sue. **Seach** (more commonly **seachad**) means 'past, alternately'. See also §3.

seachd – septet. **Seachd** is 'seven'. For the English **p** see §20.

sean – <u>sen</u>ile. **Sean** means 'old'.

seasg – sedge. Sedge grows on wet ground and **seasgann** is 'a marsh, fen', a word which appears in Shiskine, a village in the south-west of Arran.

teach – <u>teg</u>ula. **Teach** means 'house', and tegula is a roof tile. See §23.

Not surprisingly, Gaelic uses **ea** or **èa** for **e** also in borrowed words, so

beannachd – benediction. Borrowed from Latin. See §6 and §19.

gead – ged. Both words mean 'pike' (fish), and are borrowed from Norse. As in the case of the word pike itself, the reference is to the pointed, spear-shaped jaw of the fish.

peacadh – impeccable. **Peacadh** means 'sin'. Borrowed from Latin.

tèarmann – terminus. **Tèarmann** means 'sanctuary'. Borrowed from Latin. The idea is that of the limits of church territory beyond which fugitives might expect to be protected from pursuers. Tillytarmont, **Tulach an Tèarmainn** 'Sanctuary Hill', is about seven miles east of Keith. A more common word for sanctuary is **comraich**, found in the Gaelic name for Applecross, **A' Chomraich**, and Comrie in Perthshire and Fife, and elsewhere.

§35 EI AS ENGLISH E

This, with **èi**, is another combination which frequently appears as **e** in related English words, again due to a reluctance to have the letter **e** by itself inside a word without another vowel along with it. So **deich** 'ten' – '<u>dec</u>ade'. Other instances are:

beir – bear. Both words mean '(to) bear', the earlier English form being *beran*. This is the origin of the common **in<u>bh</u>ir** 'inver', i.e. a carrying into (of one river into another, or into the sea), a confluence, frequent on the west coast. See also **eileatrom** §10.

beithe – <u>bet</u>ula. **Beithe** is 'birch' and betula is a botanical term for the birch family. The word is quite common in placenames, as Aultbea, **An t-Allt Beithe** 'the Birch Stream' on Loch Ewe in Wester Ross.

ceil – hell. **Ceil** means '(to) hide'. Hell is regarded as a hidden, covered place. For the intial **c** see §2.

creid – credo, creed. **Creid** means 'believe'.

<u>deimhinne</u> – deem. **Deimhinne** means 'certain'. The idea is 'judged decisive, definite'. There is also the possibility, however, that the initial *de-* is a negative prefix and the idea is 'unchanged, unwavering'.

eilid – eland, elaphine, elk. **Eilid** is 'a hind'. Loch Eilt is a few miles west of Glenfinnan.

èirig – eric. **Èirig** is 'a ransom, reparation' and eric, in old Irish law, was a fine paid by a murderer to the victim's family. The English is borrowed. Compare wer(e)gild in §9.

greigh – <u>greg</u>arious, egregious. **Greigh** is 'a herd'.

meidh – mete, meter. **Meidh** is 'a scale, a balance'.

seiche – sec<u>t</u>ion, di<u>ssec</u>t, <u>secat</u>eurs. **Seiche** is 'a skin, hide' (of an animal) after being cut off.

Again, this occurs regularly in borrowed words, as:

cèir – cere(cloth), ceresin. **Cèir** is 'wax'. All borrowed from Latin.

clèireach – cleric. Borrowed from Latin.

deisciobal – disciple. Borrowed from Latin.

eisimpleir – example. Borrowed from Latin. For the Gaelic **s** see §22.

rèilig – relic. **Rèilig** is 'a church(yard), burial ground'. Borrowed from Latin. **Rèilig Òdhrain** 'St Oran's Chapel' is a well-known building on Iona.

sgeilp – shelf. Borrowed from Scots. See also §26.

sgeir – skerry. Borrowed from Norse.

sprèidh – <u>pred</u>atory. **Sprèidh** means 'cattle'. For the initial **s** and the reference to cattle raiding see §23. Borrowed from Latin.

teirm – term (time). Borrowed from English.

teisteanas – testimony. Borrowed from Latin.

§36 I AS ENGLISH E

This, with **ì**, is found as **e** in related English words. So **cridhe** – 'heart', Scots *hert*. For the Gaelic **c** see §2. Other instances are:

fìor – v̱e̱rify, very, aver. **Fìor** means 'true'. For the Gaelic **f** see also §9.

geimheal – gyve (earlier *giv̱e*). Both words mean 'fetter, a shackle', the English now archaic. Its origin is unclear, but the fact that the **g** was originally hard – sometimes written *guiv̱e* – suggests a connection with **geimheal**.

gin – gene. **Gin** means '(to) beget, generate'. Other cognates range from 'genetic' to 'genius', including the slightly disguised 'beniḡn' and 'maliḡn'.

gionach – genial, chin. **Gionach** is 'greedy, gluttonous' and genial is a classical cognate with the meaning 'of the chin'. The idea is 'stuffing one's face'. See also §13.

lighiche – leech. **Lighiche** means 'a doctor', as did the now obsolete 'leech', though the word remains in use in the surname Leitch. The **ee** diphthong of the English, giving a sound similar to the Gaelic **i**, is a modern spelling.

lìon – plenty, rep̱le̱nish. **Lìon** means '(to) fill'. For the Gaelic missing **p** see §20. Related also is **linn** in the sense of a full span (of time), now meaning 'a century, era, age'.

miann – mean. **Miann** is 'desire, intention'.

mil – m̱e̱llifluent. **Mil** means 'honey'. Different vowels appear in the cognates m̱i̱ldew, m̱o̱lasses and ma̱ṟmalade.

mìos – mensual. **Mìos** means 'month'. The accent on the **ì** indicates a long vowel sound, to compensate for the dropping of the **n**, as also in **cìs** below. See §19.

I AS ENGLISH E

mire – merry. **Mire** means 'fun, sport' but its etymology is unclear. The Gaelic adjective is **mear** 'merry'. Cognate also is 'mirth'. In early Irish the meaning was 'mad' and its modern sense echoes that of English, where mad, madcap etc can mean enthusiastically playful, frolicsome, like the theatrical Follies which signify fun and games. **Gille-mirein** is a spinning top, or a puppet.

rìgh – regal. **Rìgh** means 'king'. The word possibly occurs in Portree in Skye, **Port Rìgh** 'King's Port'. **Rìgh** is also related to German *Reich*, found in English as a suffix, e.g. bishop<u>ric</u>, a bishop's 'kingdom', and to names of Germanic origin as Frede<u>rick</u>, Rode<u>rick</u> etc. Cognate also is 'rich', originally referring to a great landowner.

<u>sinn</u>sear – <u>sen</u>ate, <u>sen</u>ior, <u>sen</u>ile. **Sinnsear** means 'ancestors'. The root of the word is **sean** 'old'.

sìth – settle, sedate. **Sìth** means 'peace'. The idea is 'at peace, settled'.

tìr – <u>terr</u>ain, terrier, in<u>ter</u> (i.e. bury) etc. **Tìr** means 'land'. It occurs in several placenames, notably Tiree, **Tiriodh** 'Corn Land'. Also related are the *earth*enware tureen, and terrine, its contents. The word also occurs in **oitir** 'outland', a low sandbank or similar extending out into the sea. It is anglicised as *otter*, hence Otter Ferry on the east coast of Loch Fyne. The idea is <u>dry</u> land; related is **tioram** 'dry'. The roofless walls of Castle Tioram in Moidart, at the end of a **dòirlinn**, can be reached on dry land except at high tide. See also **tart** §28.

Borrowings include:

cill – cell. **Cill** means 'church(yard)', and was earlier a monastic cell. It is very common in placenames, anglicised as kil, keil and kel; there are dozens of examples of kil- places, as Kilbride, **Cill Bhrìghde**, 'St Bridget's Church' in Argyll and other areas. Borrowed from Latin. See also **ceall** §2.

cìs – <u>cens</u>us. **Cìs** means 'a tax', one of the results of a census. Borrowed from Latin. See also §19.

clìceach – cleekie. **Clìceach** means 'cunning, underhand'. Borrowed from Scots.

dìblidh – debilitated. **Dìblidh** means 'wretched, in poor condition'. Borrowed from Latin (as is the English), with the Gaelic accent on the first syllable reflecting a long vowel in the Latin word.

litir – letter. Borrowed from Latin.

riaghailt – regulation. Borrowed from Latin.

§37 O AS ENGLISH U

A Gaelic **o** or **ò** is often found where a related English word has **u**. This is a regular change in Gaelic itself, as **bòrd** 'table', **bùird** 'tables'. So **boc** 'a male deer or goat' is related to English 'buck, butcher'. Several placenames contain the word, notably (probably) Buckie, on the coast just east of Elgin; there is also a Glen Buckie in Perthshire.

Other words with this feature are:

bòc – buccal, saltimbocca. **Bòc** means 'swell, inflate' and buccal refers to the (swollen, puffed) cheeks. In the modern Romance languages the word now means 'mouth', hence the Italian savoury dish saltimbocca.

bòcan – bug(bear), Puck. **Bòcan** is 'a hobgoblin, a mischievous fairy', and bug is an old word for an evil spectre. Puck, on the other hand, was a more playful fairy.

cnò – nut. See §2.

dòcha – conducive, and all the -duc(t) compounds, dux and duke. **Dòcha** means 'probable, likely'; the idea is 'leading (to)'. From the same source is **dòchas** 'hope'. The Gaelic accent reflects a long vowel in the Latin root.

donn – dun. **Donn** means 'brown'. This is the origin of the surnames Duncan and Donachie, as well as some instances of Dunn.

goile – gullet. **Goile** means 'stomach, throat'. Also related, with metathesis, is 'glutton'.

lòchran – lucid, lucifer. **Lòchran** means 'a light, lantern'. See also **luachair** §39.

loth – lute. **Loth** means 'a marsh, mud', and lute is a mixture of clay and cement used for sealing joints. The word occurs in the East Sutherland coastal villages of Lothmore and Lothbeg, which share this etymology, if little else, with Paris. The French capital was originally called Lutetia, 'mud town', and also gave its name to lutetium, a metallic element discovered last century by a Parisian scientist.

òg – young, Junker. For the missing **n** in Gaelic see §19.

olc – ulcer. **Olc** means 'bad'. The idea is 'wound', both literally and figuratively. Also related is the medical term helcoid, meaning 'ulcerous'.

òr – auric. **Òr** is 'gold', and the various aur- compounds refer to the colour yellow. 'Or' is also a heraldic term indicating gold engraving etc.

òtrach – putrid. **Òtrach** is 'a dung-heap'. For the missing **p** see §20.

ronn – run. **Ronn** is 'mucus'. A runny nose.

sònraichte – (a)sunder. **Sònraichte** means 'special, particular'. The idea is 'being apart from, different'. For the disappearance of the **d** in the Gaelic see §19; a double **n** would be expected to compensate for the lost **d** and it appears in the earlier Irish form *sunnraid*.

tom – tumulus. **Tom** is 'a hillock'. In tumulus 'burial mound' the Latin *-ulus* ending indicates a diminutive, a feature found also in Scots *tummock*, borrowed from Gaelic. Also cognate is English 'tomb'. **Tom** is common in placenames, as Tomatin, **Tom Aitinn** 'Juniper Hillock', about a dozen miles south-east of Inverness. See also **tuam** §39.

Borrowings showing this vowel alternation include:

clòimh – plume. **Clòimh** means 'wool'. Borrowed from Latin. For the Gaelic **c** see §5.

còrcair – purple. Also **corcair**. Borrowed from Latin. For the Gaelic **c** see §5.

croch – crucify. **Croch** means '(to) hang'. Borrowed from Latin. Also cognate is English 'cross'.

dròaid – drugget. Drugget is a coarse fabric of linen and wool, often used as a rug. Borrowed from English.

rong – rung. Borrowed from English.

smodal – smut. **Smodal** is 'trash, crumbs, fragments'. Borrowed from English 'smut', possibly influenced by Scots *smot* – a dark mark (on a sheep for identification).

sòrn – furnace. **Sòrn** is 'a flue'. Borrowed from Latin. For the **s** see §21.

spong – fungus. **Spong** means 'tinder'. Borrowed from Latin. For the **s** see §21.

spor – spur. Borrowed from English.

sporan – purse, bursar. Borrowed from Latin. For the **s** see §23.

tonnag – tunic. **Tonnag** means 'a shawl'. Borrowed from Latin.

trombaid – trumpet. Borrowed from English. Related is **tromb**, 'trump, Jew's harp'. For the Gaelic **b** see §1.

§38 U AS ENGLISH O

A Gaelic **u** or **ù** is often found where a related English word has **o**. So **muir** 'sea' appears in cor<u>mor</u>ant 'sea crow', the placename Moray 'Sea Settlement' and the surname Morgan. The Gaelic vowel remains, however, in Murray, Murphy, Murdoch, Murchison etc. Other words with this vowel change include:

cruinn – crown. **Cruinn** means 'round'. Hence also **cruinnich** 'gather', i.e. <u>round</u> up. Also related are 'corona, curve'.

cuid – quota. **Cuid** means 'a part, share'. For the Gaelic **c** see §3.

cuileann – holly. For the Gaelic **c** see §2.

cuimhne – <u>comm</u>emorate. **Cuimhne** means 'memory'. Both words contain the common prefix com- (con, co), 'with, together', but here Gaelic has the (Latin) form *cum*, which English never does. Also related to **cuimhne** are 'mind, mental, mention, reminisce' etc.

cuing – <u>conj</u>ugal, <u>conjunc</u>tion. **Cuing** is 'a yoke'. For the prefix cu- see the preceding word. Also probably related is Scots *jougs* (earlier *jokkis*), an iron collar and chain by which offenders were tied to a wall or post.

cùl – re<u>coil</u>. **Cùl** means 'back'. Also cognate are some French-based terms, as *cul de sac*, a lane closed off at the bottom, a blind alley. The word is quite common in placenames, the best known probably being <u>Coul</u>port on Loch Long, opposite Ardentinny.

curach – coracle.

duais – dose. **Duais** is 'a prize, reward'. A dose is 'something given'. Also related is 'donation', see **dàn** §31.

U AS ENGLISH O

muineal – <u>monile</u>form, mane. **Muineal** means 'neck', and monileform means 'like a necklace, string of beads'. Also related is **muing** 'mane' (of a horse).

sùil – solar. **Sùil** means 'an eye', the idea being that the sun is the eye in the sky. Also related are the many helio- (sun) compounds, as explained in §24.

tuath – <u>to</u>tal. **Tuath** is the tenantry, or what used to be called peasantry, country dwellers. The reference is to their vast numbers compared with the nobility. This is the origin of the famous Welsh name <u>Tud</u>or, as well as <u>Teut</u>onic and <u>Dut</u>ch, all meaning 'people(s)'. The same idea is possibly to be found in plebs, plebeian (English cognates 'plenty, plethora, pleonasm'), relating to the masses as opposed to the relatively few patricians. Another English cognate, 'full', shows the alternation between **p** and **f** mentioned above in §20.

tùs – Macin<u>tosh</u>. **Tùs** means 'beginning', and **Mac an Tòisich** means 'Son of the Leader', the related **toiseach** also meaning 'beginning, leading off'.

ugh – oval, ovary. **Ugh** is 'an egg'. The word was formerly spelled **ubh**, which better suits 'oval', but the modern spelling **ugh** better suits another cognate, 'egg'.

uidh – <u>pod</u>ium, <u>pod</u>agra. **Uidh** is 'a journey, stage' (originally on foot), commonly heard in **ceann-uidhe**, 'journey's end, destination'. Podagra is 'gout' (of the foot). For the missing **p** see §20.

<u>uirc</u>ean – pork. **Uircean** is 'a piglet'. For the missing **p** see §20.

Borrowings with this feature include:

cùis – chose, Cosa Nostra. **Cùis** means 'a matter, affair', and 'chose' is a legal term meaning 'a thing, a piece of property'. Cosa Nostra 'Our Thing' is an organisation of the Mafia. Also related is

English 'cause', where the vowel has an open **o** sound. Borrowed from Latin.

cùmhnant – covenant. **Cùmhnant** means 'a contract'. Borrowed from Scots. The **mh** is not sounded (though its nasalising effect is preserved) and is a 'learned' insertion for reasons of etymology; compare **sgriubha** §13 and contrast §30. It was neither written nor sounded in Scots *cunnand* (various spellings).

dùsal – doze (slumber). Borrowed from English, or Norse.

muileann – molar. **Muileann** is 'a mill', and molar means 'grinding'; as a noun it refers to the grinding tooth. Common in placenames, as Lagavulin, **Lag a' Mhuilinn** 'Hollow of the Mill' on Islay. Borrowed from Latin.

sguab – scopa. **Sguab** is 'a brush' and scopa is a bundle of hairs on the legs of bees for collecting pollen. Borrowed from the Latin word for a brush of twigs, a besom.

spùill – spoil. Borrowed from a Scots form *spulyie* (various spellings) of English 'spoil' (to plunder). Another form is **spùinn**, and **spùinneadair** is in common use for a pirate.

sùlaire – solan (goose, i.e. gannet). Borrowed from Norse. The young of this bird, known in Gaelic as **guga**, is caught and eaten by inhabitants of Ness, at the north end of Lewis. The birds are caught during August on Sulasgeir 'Solan Skerry', an uninhabited rocky island about 60 miles north of Lewis.

uinnean – onion. Borrowed from English, via Norman French. Ultimately from the Latin word for 'one' (see **aon** §32), an apparent reference to the single bulb of several cloves or layers.

§39 UA AS ENGLISH U

This combination, where both vowels are sounded, is often found where related English words have just **u**, or its sound. So **buachaille** 'a herdsman, cowherd' is cognate with 'bucolic'. The main root of the word is **bò** 'cow' (English 'bovine'). **Buachaille Èite Mòr** (and **Beag**) are well-known mountains at the head of Glen Etive near Glencoe. Other words with this feature are:

bruadar – frustrate, fraud(ulent). **Bruadar** is 'a dream'. The idea is that dreams cheat you, they're not real. For the initial **b/f** interchange see under **bonn** §19. There is some doubt in this instance because the precise origin of Latin *fraus* (English fraud etc) is not certain, but initial Indo-European **dh** often became **f** in Latin and **b** in English and Gaelic. Bruadar is also a male forename (the noun is masculine in Gaelic), much less common than Aisling or Ashling, a female forename (from another 'dream' word, **aisling**, a feminine noun). This may be because of some folk-memory of the more positive associations of the latter – it means 'outstanding, ecstatic, extraordinary' – compared to the rather pejorative **bruadar**, though such considerations would be unlikely to affect either word's usage today. Native Gaelic male and female forenames tend to derive from masculine and feminine nouns respectively. A placename from the forename is Drumbroider near Falkirk.

buaidh – Boudicca. **Buaidh** means 'victory', and Boudicca ('victorious') was a warlike queen of the Iceni in East Anglia in the Ist century A.D. during the Roman occupation. An alternative English form of her name, Boadicea, has the Gaelic **a**, but this seems coincidental, since there was no **a** in the Old British and Welsh forms of **buaidh**.

cruaidh – crude. **Cruaidh** means 'hard'. Kerrycroy, **An Ceathramh Cruaidh**, on Bute, is 'the Hard Quarterland', i.e. a quarter of a davach, an area of land used for tax assessment. See also **cruaidh** §2.

GAELIC AND ENGLISH

luach – lucre, lucrative. **Luach** means 'value, worth'. Also related is **lurach** 'beautiful'; Gaelic regularly drops an Indo-European **c** before **r**, though a long vowel, **lùrach**, would be normal as compensation. There is also connection with **leòr** 'plenty' §30.

luachair – lucid, lucifer. **Luachair** is '(bul)rush', the pith of which was formerly used to make a sort of candle. The word appears in Leuchars, Fife. See also **lòchran** §37.

nuadh – new. The English word has a **u** or **oo**, sound, of course, especially in America.

ruadh – ruddy. **Ruadh** is 'red, reddish-brown'. Anglicised 'roy', as in Rob Roy MacGregor, the infamous highland outlaw and folk hero. Common in placenames, as Glen Roy (of the parallel roads) north-east of Spean Bridge. Cognate also are of course 'red' and the surname Reid.

truagh – drudge. **Truagh** means 'wretched'. Compare also Scots *trauchle*. The word occurs also in **tròcair** 'mercy' (i.e. affection for the wretched).

truaill – intrude. **Truaill** is 'a sheath, scabbard'. The idea is 'thrust into'. See also §28.

uabhar – hubris. Both words mean 'arrogance, overweening pride'.

Borrowings are:

cnuas – crush. **Cnuas** mean 'chew, crunch, ponder' (chew over). This derivation from English is not certain, however, and is based on the fact that initial **cn** is usually sounded **cr** in Gaelic.

luan – lunar. **Luan** is an old word for 'moon' (modern Gaelic **gealach** – see §34), but is in everyday use in **Diluain** 'Monday' – i.e. moon day, as in other European languages, e.g. *lunedì*, *lundi* etc. Borrowed from Latin.

UA AS ENGLISH U

tuam – tomb. The English sound is **u** or **oo**, of course. Borrowed from Late Latin or English.

§40 METATHESIS

Finally, some miscellaneous features.

This exchange of places between letters of a word has been explained in the introduction, and several examples have been given above, viz. **call**, **cridhe**, **crodh**, **cruimh** (all §2), **druid** (§7), **raineach** (§10), **gruth** (§13) and **sporan** (§23). To these can be added the following:

aingeal – ignite, ingle. **Aingeal** meant – it is seldom used today – 'fire'.

beurla – **port-à-beul**. The latter, meaning 'mouth music', is of course Gaelic but is probably well enough known to illustrate the metathesis. **Beul** means 'mouth', and **beurla** is the English language. The idea is 'mouthings, speech', the only other non-Gaelic relevant speech being English.

bleoghain(n) – milk. **Bleoghain(n)** is '(to) milk' (milk itself is **bainne**). The Gaelic and English words illustrate the close connection between **b** and **m** – both are bilabials – found in many languages. Because the lips close, as if forming an **m**, before making a **b** sound, this **m** is frequently followed by a **b** which has been added unnecessarily. As mentioned above under **imleag** §13, the word *number* shouldn't have a **b**, since it wasn't there in the Indo-European root, as the related word *numeral* indicates. As for an unnecessary **m**, consider the Gaelic borrowing **tombaca** from English tobacco. Apart from the obvious historical reason, you can tell that this is a borrowing since original Gaelic words no longer permit the combination **mb** (see under **imleag** §13). As a result there are Gaelic words today which can start with a **b** or an **m**, according to the dialect, and words which now begin with a **b** started with an **m** in Middle and Old Irish. This is still a feature of Irish today, so that, for instance, Gaelic **bòid** 'a vow' is Irish *móid*. This is related to a feature called eclipsis where an initial **b** changes to an **m** in Irish – and in Welsh, the nasal mutation - for various

METATHESIS

grammatical reasons.[34] This is also what lies behind Gaelic **mnathan** as the plural of **bean** 'wife, woman', and explains why 'morning' is *bore* in Welsh (compare archaic English morrow and Gaelic **màireach**). So Munlochy in the Black Isle is from earlier **Bun Lòchaidh**; possibly compare also, in the Indo- side of Indo-European, Bombay and its modern form Mumbai. See also **mannas** §19 above. The Gaelic vowels in **bleoghain(n)** appear in the Old English form of milk, *meolc*, and the metathesis is a feature of some Slav languages, as Polish *mleko* 'milk'. For the Gaelic **g** but English **k** see §13.

breith – birth. The related **beir**, 'give birth' is more like the English and its cognates 'bear, born, bairn' etc.

bris(**t**) – burst. **Bris**(**t**) means '(to) break'. The word appears in **Eilean Druim Briste** 'Island of the Broken Ridge', a Gaelic name for Bottle Island, at the entrance to Loch Broom. The English name apparently refers to the shape of the island.

corc – kukri. **Corc** is 'a knife, cleaver' and a kukri is a large curved knife used by Gurkhas., whose language was Indo-European.

dearbh – true. **Dearbh** means 'certain, sure, exact'. For the Gaelic **d** see §7.

ionga – nail, unguis. All words refer to a nail (of the finger or toe). The missing **g** in nail was there in Old English *nægl* (various spellings, but all with **g**; the **l** signifies a diminutive in English). Unguis is a classical cognate from Latin.

làmh – palm. **Làmh** means 'hand'. For the missing **p** see §20. The word appears in **ullamh** 'ready, to hand'.

leamhan – elm. Classical cognates are 'ulmin', a gum which exudes from elm trees, and 'ulmaceous' (elm-like). The word occurs

---

[34] It's also an 'unofficial' feature of Gaelic in some areas, e.g. Lewis.

in several placenames, notably Vale of Leven, **Magh Leamhna** in Lennox, **An Leamhnachd**, an area to the east of Loch Lomond, Aberlemno in Angus, and in England <u>Leam</u>ington Spa. It should be added, though, that Leven elsewhere (a couple of rivers and lochs in Scotland and a couple of villages in England) could possibly mean "smooth" or "liable to flooding".

mislean – molasses. **Mislean** is 'sweet meadow grass', from **milis** 'sweet'.

slàn – <u>sal</u>ve, <u>sal</u>vo, <u>sal</u>ute, sage (the healing plant, **slàn-lus**). The general sense is 'good health', and this is what lies behind its extended Gaelic use as 'farewell, goodbye'.

sreath – series.

tàirneanach – Tanar. **Tàirneanach** is 'thunder', and refers to the thunderous flow of the River Tanar in Aberdeenshire. See also §28.

Borrowings with this feature are:

asgaill – axil, axilla. **Asgaill** means 'armpit, oxter', as does the medical term axilla. Axil is a botanical term for the armpit-like area between the leaf and stem of a plant. Borrowed from Latin. The more common word is **achlais**, but **asgaill** is used in some areas, e.g. Islay.

baist – baptise. Borrowed from Latin. For the missing **p** see §20.

cistin – kitchen. Borrowed from English. A more common form **cidsin** is closer to the English.

còisir – chorus. **Còisir** means 'choir', another cognate. Borrowed from Latin.

coisrig – consecrate. Borrowed from Latin. For the Gaelic **g** see §13.

Metathesis

easbaig – epis<u>c</u>opal. **Easbaig** means 'bishop'. Borrowed from Latin. The word, always with the metathesis, occurs in a few placenames, as Balnespick, a few miles north of Kingussie, and in the surname Macanespie.

easbaloid – absolution. Borrowed from Latin.

goistidh – gossip. **Goistidh** is 'a godparent'. The Gaelic was until recently written **goisdidh**, which better illustrates the metathesis (d/s) with the earlier English *godsib*, from which the Gaelic was borrowed. Godsib was a godparent (*sib* as in <u>sib</u>ling) and later signified a familiar friend with whom one might chat or gossip, hence its meaning today. The sense of **goistidh** has also evolved, and now has the additional meaning of 'a sponsor'.

pàiste – page(boy). **Pàiste** is a young child. Borrowed from English.

rùda – hurt. **Rùda** is 'a ram' and the original idea of 'hurt' (borrowed from French) was to ram into, to knock against. Borrowed from Norse.

sporan – purse. Borrowed from Latin. It is possible, however, that the **s** in Gaelic is simply an unnecessary addition, something which occurs quite often in both Gaelic and English (see §23).

stang – sta<u>g</u>nate. **Stang** is 'a ditch, pool'. Borrowed from Scots *stank* with the same meaning. Ultimately from Latin.

susbaint – substance. Borrowed from Latin or English.

trosg – torsk. Both words mean 'cod(fish)'. Borrowed from Norse; the Norse form appears (with a vowel change, see §31) in Tarskavaig 'Cod Bay' in the Sleat peninsula, Skye.

§41 EXTRA VOWEL AND SCHWA

An additional unwritten vowel sound between Gaelic consonants. This is a prominent feature of Gaelic, and it is also a feature of Scots, as 'film', pronounced *filum*, 'umbrella' pronounced *umberella* and so on. Grammar books sometimes refer to it as the svarabhakti vowel from its prominence in Sanskrit. In the past this extra vowel has sometimes been written in Gaelic words, but the instances listed below reflect current spelling. In borrowed words the added vowel sound may echo the original; so **cainb** and 'canna<u>b</u>is' (see §2). Or it may not; **arm** 'army' is pronounced something like *aram*, and 'the army' is **an t-arm**, which doesn't sound much like the English at all. Words with this feature include:

ainm – an<u>onym</u>ous, <u>onom</u>atopoeia, <u>onom</u>astic, patr<u>onym</u>ic. **Ainm** means 'name', another cognate, along with 'nominate', and 'noun'.

calman – columbine, Columba. **Calman** means 'dove'. It is the origin of the names Calum, Malcolm, MacCallum etc and of places named after St Columba, as Iona, **Ì Chaluim Chille**.

colbh – column.

seanchaidh – seannachie. Both words mean 'a story-teller', a reciter of genealogy and clan lore. The Gaelic is the source, based on **sean** 'old' – see §26, §34, §36.

§42 Miscellaneous

Finally, some fairly common Gaelic words which don't fit easily into any of the above categories, and related words in English:

aghann – an<u>gio</u>gram. **Aghann** is 'a pan, vessel, small container'. Medical terms with angio- refer to blood vessels, and are a classical cognate. A difficulty, however, is the missing **n** before the **g** in the Gaelic, since it is retained in native words such as **cumhang** 'narrow', though usually at the end of a word or root, unlike **aghann**.

aiteann – edge. **Aiteann** is 'juniper'. The idea is that of sharpness, referring to the shrub's prickly needle-like leaves. Found in one or two placenames, as Tomatin, **Tom Aitinn**, about a dozen miles south-east of Inverness.

allt – <u>alt</u>itude. **Allt** is 'a stream, burn'. The idea is that of a high mountain stream; **allt** was a precipice or height in earlier Gaelic and Welsh *allt* is a hillside, cliff. Common in placenames.

altram – <u>alt</u>rices, <u>a</u>limony, <u>a</u>liment. **Altram** means 'nourishing, fostering', and altrices are prematurely hatched birds requiring much nourishment. **Banaltram** is a (female) nurse. Also cognate is 'old' (i.e. nourished, fully grown) and, ultimately, the various alt- compounds, as 'altitude, alto' (originally a counter-tenor, the highest male voice) with sense of 'raised up'.

arbhar – arval, ar<u>v</u>icola. **Arbhar** is 'corn' and arvicola is a term for a species of voles (field dwellers). The general idea is a ploughed field. Ardnarff **Àird an Arbha(ir)**, 'Promontory of the Corn' is on the south side of Loch Carron, just east of Strome Ferry. Related also is the now rarely used **àr** 'ploughing', with its cognate arable. The accent is puzzling, since it wasn't there in the Indo-European source, but the earlier Irish form was *ar*.

bachall – bacillus. **Bachall** is 'a rod, crozier' and bacillus is a rod-shaped bacterium.

balg – bulge, belly, bellows. **Balg** is 'a bag'. The idea is 'swelling'.

binn – ban, banns. **Binn** is 'a verdict, a sentence', and ban is a proclamation, condemnation; banns are an announcement of a forthcoming marriage.

brìgh – brio. **Brìgh** is 'energy' and the words *con brio* (energetically, with spirit), though Italian, are part of the international language of music. The word entered Italian from Spanish in the sixteenth century and is generally regarded as being of Celtic origin. A Celtic language was still spoken in Spain long after its subjugation by the Roman Empire.

brod – brad(awl), em<u>broid</u>er. **Brod** is 'a goad'. Also related is **<u>bros</u>naich** '(to) incite, spur'. The general idea in all this is 'to needle', literally and figuratively.

brù – em<u>bryo</u>. **Brù** means 'belly, womb'. For the prefix in English compare **rùchd** §6, and **còrd**, **liubhair** in this section.

brùth – bruise.

buidhe – bay. **Buidhe** means 'yellow', and bay is reddish-brown, the colour of chestnut. The botanical classical cognate 'badious' shows the **d** of the Gaelic, unlike 'bay' which has come through French. The word appears in several placenames, as Lochbuie in the south of Mull, and in the surname Bowie, presumably referring originally to flaxen hair.

car – curve. **Car** is 'a twist, turn'.

carrasan – coryza. Both words mean 'catarrh'.

clàr – clerk, clergy. **Clàr** is 'a flat surface, a table' (of events, dates etc). The word clergy comes from a Greek word for 'a lot, destiny' originally determined by drawing a piece of wood. The modern meanings of **clàr** have diverged considerably from this, but the accent reflects a long vowel in the Greek.

MISCELLANEOUS

coire – corrie. **Coire** is 'a cauldron, kettle', and a corrie is a cauldron-shaped hollow in a hill, as in Corrour on Loch Ossian north of Rannoch. It can also mean 'whirlpool', as in the famous Corryvreckan between Scarba and Jura.

connlach – cannula, cannelloni. **Connlach** is 'straw', and a cannula is a surgical breathing tube, while cannelloni are stuffed macaroni.

cuilc – <u>cal</u>amus. **Cuilc** is 'a reed, cane', and calamus is a straw or reed and a type of palm from which rattan canes are made.

cuileag – culex. **Cuileag** is 'a fly', of the culex genus familiar to entomologists. The word has found a new use as a cursor on computer monitor screens.

cullach – cullion. **Cullach** is 'an (uncastrated) boar', and cullion is an abusive term for a wretch, scum, now mainly Scots. The English is from a French word for a testicle - formerly its meaning in English too - and this is also the root of **cullach**. For the sense compare balls (rubbish), balls-up (a botched mess).

cuman – cymbal, coomb. **Cuman** is 'a (milking) pail'. Coomb is 'a valley, a hollow', common in many Welsh and English placenames, as in the well-known hymn tune *Cwm Rhondda*. The idea is of a curved shape. For the **b** missing from the Gaelic see **imleag** §13.

cumhang – anguish, <u>angu</u>stifoliate. **Cumhang** means 'narrow' and the original idea of anguish was a choking tightness; angustifoliate describes plants with narrow leaves.

dàil – dwell. **Dàil** means 'delay'. The sense is 'stay', i.e. restrain.

dàimh – <u>demo</u>cracy. **Dàimh** means 'relationship, kinship'. The idea is that of a people or tribe.

dall – dull. **Dall** means 'blind'.

GAELIC AND ENGLISH

(an)-diugh – diurnal, journal, so<u>journ</u>. **An-diugh** means 'today'; **an** is the definite article as in Scots *the day* (i.e. today). Diurnal is a classical cognate meaning 'daily' and a journal (compare French *jour*) was originally a daily record. The Gaelic **d** echoes the sound of the **j**. The **gh** of **an-diugh** is an unnecessary modern suffix (not pronounced); the earlier form was **an diu**, and the **gh** doesn't appear in this word in the other Celtic languages.

donnal – din. **Donnal** means 'a howl'.

eàrr – arse, wheat<u>ear</u>. **Eàrr** means 'a tail'. The loss of Indo-European **s** after **r**, resulting in double **r**, is a regular feature of Gaelic. Wheat<u>ear</u> (i.e. white arse) is a bird with a white rump. From a related Greek word comes squ<u>irrel</u> (its tail being its most prominent feature). Classical cognates are <u>ouro</u>boros, a snake or dragon of mythology always depicted with its tail in its mouth, an ancient alchemy symbol representing the eternal cycle of renewal, and cynos<u>ure</u>, 'dog's tail', the constellation Ursa Minor.

eigh – icicle. The more usual form is **deigh**, though this is a mistake, the **d** being originally part of the definite article. You can tell this also from other ice words from the same root, as Gaelic **eighre** and Welsh *iâ*, which don't have the **d**. For a similar process in English see under **èiteag** §16, and the introduction to §29.

eile – else. **Eile** means 'other'. Classical cognates are alien, alias, alibi, alt<u>ern</u>ate, sub<u>altern</u>.

èirich – erect. **Èirich** means '(to) rise'. Also related, without the prefix, is 'right' in the sense of straight, direct.

fhuair – (h)eureka, heuristic. **Fhuair** means 'found, got', and eureka is used to signify a discovery. With a lenited **f** (**fh**) in Gaelic the **f** is not sounded.

giall – jowl. **Giall** is both 'jowl' and 'jaw'. Jowl can mean the fleshy part hanging from the jaw, or the jaw (and cheek) itself, and the two senses have different origins in Old English. This may be reflected in Gaelic, which has another spelling **ciobhal**. The **j** of jowl, however, not found in Old English, is thought to show the influence of French *joue* 'cheek', and it is interesting that the Latin word from which the French is derived has an internal **b**, as does **ciobhal**. **Giall/ciobhal** also appears in **peirceall**, another word for 'jaw'.

glas – glass. **Glas** means 'grey, greenish'. The idea of glass is 'shiny, translucent, glimmering'; early instances of glass were not the colourless transparent examples of today. Common in placenames, the most well-known being Glasgow. This is from Early Welsh, Old British, however. *Glas* can mean grey-green in modern Welsh also, but it more commonly means blue. Compare the rare and long obsolete English *glastum*, meaning woad (a blue dye), thought to be the root of Glastonbury in England.

gobhal – gable. **Gobhal** is 'a fork'. Related also is Scots (*hornie*) *gollach* 'earwig' (Gaelic **gòbhlag**). The word occurs in several placenames, Dungavel 'Forked Hill', a few miles east of Kilmarnock, being the best known.

greas – progress. **Greas** means 'hasten'.

imlich – lick. The Gaelic prefix im- means something like 'around'.

innis – inch, island. **Innis** is generally used for inland islands (e.g. on Loch Lomond) and coastal waters. It also means a grassy meadow beside a river, hence the Inches in Perth, Brechin and elsewhere.

ìobair – offer. **Ìobair** means '(to) sacrifice'. Both words have the same Indo-European root meaning 'to bring'; the Gaelic form became **beir** and the Latin *fero* and English 'offer' is based on the Latin.

ionnsaich – sagacious. **Ionnsaich** means 'learn', and sagacious is 'learned, wise'.

GAELIC AND ENGLISH

labhair – labrum, labrose. **Labhair** means 'speak', and labrum and labrose refer to lips. As in English, the word is used of a babbling brook; Lawers (village and mountain) on the north side of Loch Tay are named after a local burn, loud and noisy. Related also are the surnames Lavery and Lowry.

lèine – linen. **Lèine** is 'a shirt'. Also related are **lìon** 'flax' and the cognates lint, linoleum, crinoline, lingerie and linnet (apparently because it eats flax seeds).

leth – lateral. **Leth** means 'side'.

liagh – ligule, bilingual, linguist. **Liagh** is 'a ladle' – roughly something tongue-shaped, so also 'the blade of an oar'. Ligule (also ligula) is a classical cognate referring to a strap- or tongue-shaped part of a flower. Linguist, of course, refers to tongue in the sense of language.

lìomh – limation. **Lìomh** means 'polish' and limation is a classical cognate meaning 'filing'. The general idea is 'smoothing'. The Gaelic accent reflects the fact that the **i** is long in Latin. This is thought to be the meaning of Glen Lyon **Gleann Lìomhann** in Perthshire, from its smooth terrain.

lobh – labefaction, lapse. **Lobh** means '(to) rot, decay' and labefaction is a classical cognate of similar meaning. This is the source of the placename Lovat, at Beauly. The Lovat reference is probably to rotting seaweed, and it would be interesting to know if the later Norman-French import from England of the name Beauly (*beau lieu*, beautiful place) was an attempt to counteract the negative image of the name Lovat. There are certain similarities with the attempts of Clan Campbell in the 14th century to hint at a Norman-French ancestry (*de campo bello*, of the beautiful plain) to counteract any pejorative meaning of their name.[35] The p still remains in the English form of the name, but not in the Gaelic.

luaidh – laud. **Luaidh** means 'to mention, praise'.

lugha – light (weight). **Lugha** means 'less, smaller'. The word probably appears also in *leprechaun*, the Irish elf; the earlier form was *luchorpán* 'small body' i.e. one of the little people. Compare Gaelic **luspardan**, **luchraban** 'dwarf'.

màm – mammary. **Màm** is 'a round hill', as is another cognate 'mamelon'. Mam Ratigan (various spellings) is a well-known mountain pass between Loch Duich and Glenelg; compare also the Paps of Jura and Glencoe.

marc – mare. **Marc** means 'horse'. Also related is 'marshal' (see under **sgalag** §26). The word is fairly common, sometimes from the similar Old British *march*, in placenames, as Markinch 'Horse Meadow' in Fife, and Rosemarkie in the Black Isle.

mealbhag – malva. **Mealbhag** is 'a poppy', and malva is a botanical term for the mallow genus of plants.

meall – malice, malign, dismal, and the many *mal*- compounds. **Meall** means 'deceive, cheat'. See also **mallachd** below in this section.

mearachd – mar. **Mearachd** is 'a mistake'.

meas – mast. **Meas** means 'fruit, acorn', and mast is the nuts of various trees such as beech, oak, and chestnut. The word occurs in Innermessan, on Loch Ryan, a few miles north of Stranraer.

meil – meal, mill. **Meil** means '(to) grind'.

miosa – misfortune etc. **Miosa** means 'worse'.

---

[35] Many other clans took the name Campbell figuratively: **cam beul**, wry or crooked mouth, i.e. you couldn't trust what they said.

molach – mall<u>o</u>phaga. **Molach** means 'hairy, rough, shaggy' and mallophaga is the scientific name for bird-lice which live in the hair of creatures such as rodents, squirrels etc.

monadh – e<u>min</u>ence, mount. **Monadh** is 'high ground, uplands, mountain range'. The Monadhliath mountain range runs east of Loch Ness, and Moncrieff (**Monadh Craoibhe** 'Hill of the Tree') is just south of Perth.

monais – re<u>main</u>, manse, manor, per<u>man</u>ent. **Monais** means 'slowness, negligence, dullness'. The idea is that of tardiness, staying put, not moving on. More common is the adjective **monaiseach** 'dull, slow-witted, unpretentious'.

mòr – more. **Mòr** means 'big'. 'More' is of course the comparative (i.e. *bigger*), and was earlier 'mo' (hence the superlative *mo-est*, now 'most'). The Gaelic comparative is **mò** 'bigger'.

mult – mutton. **Mult** is 'a wether, a castrated ram'. Also **molt**.

mùr – myriad. **Mùr** is 'a very large, countless number'. The Gaelic accent reflects the long vowel in the Indo-European root, and is further evidence that the word is unlikely to have been borrowed from English, where the y in myriad is a short vowel.

nàmhaid – nemesis. **Nàmhaid** is 'an enemy', and Nemesis is the Greek goddess of vengeance. In modern English it is used to mean an agent of retribution and vengeance.

neul – nebula, nebulous. **Neul** is 'a cloud'. The related French *nuage* and *nue* also lose the **b** from Latin as usual; it was never there in Gaelic or Irish but the long **eu** diphthong compensates for its absence. For a similar feature in a Gaelic borrowing see **tàileasg** below. Strathnaver in Sutherland (with river and inver) is also thought to have a similar meaning, perhaps referring to mist in the glen or on the river, but this would be from Old British, not Gaelic; compare modern Welsh *nifwl* 'mist, fog'. Also cognate is nuance (via French *nuage* mentioned above), the idea being 'shade, subtlety'.

MISCELLANEOUS

nochd – naked. Nochty Burn, about 5 miles east of the Lecht ski centre, and Naked Tam (Tom Nochd), a hill about ten miles west of Brechin, Angus, both presumably refer to a lack of vegetation.

oir – orarian. **Oir** means 'edge, border' and orarian is a classical cognate referring to the shoreline.

olann – lanate, lanose. **Olann** is 'wool'.

ràmh – tri<u>reme</u>. **Ràmh** is 'an oar'. The same root appears in **iorram** 'boat song', sung at the oars. Dundarave Castle at the head of Loch Fyne is thought to be **Dùn Dà Ràmh** 'Hill Fort of Two Oars', but the reason is obscure.

riasg – rush. **Riasg** is 'sedge, marshy ground', and rush was *risce* in Old English. Riasg Buidhe was a village on Colonsay, abandoned in 1918 when the inhabitants moved to nearby Glasard.

roth – <u>rot</u>ate. **Roth** is 'a wheel'. Cognate also is Gaelic **ruith** 'run' and English roll, round, and rotund; rotund keeps the **t** because it was borrowed from Latin, whereas round was borrowed from French, which as usual (*père* / *pa<u>t</u>er* etc) dropped the Latin **t**.

rùn – rune. **Rùn** means 'a secret, mystery', and a rune is a character of an ancient Germanic alphabet thought to have magical significance.

sail – <u>shill</u>elagh. **Sail** is 'a beam, log'. A shillelagh is a heavy wooden cudgel usually of oak or blackthorn, and thought to have been named after a wood of oaks in County Wicklow, which in turn would have been formed from **sail**.

salach – sallow. **Salach** means 'dirty'. Sallow is 'pale, off colour', related to French *sale* 'dirty'.

samhail – similar, same.

samhradh – summer. Also related may be **samhain** (November), with a reference to the end of summer. Dwelly's dictionary records **samh** with the rare meaning 'sun', a relic of earlier Irish (obsolete in modern Gaelic). The word occurs in a few placenames, notably **Na h-Eileanan Samhraidh** 'The Summer Isles' at the entrance to Loch Broom, Ross & Cromarty.

sàth – satisfy. **Sàth** means 'plenty, enough'.

searbh – sour.

seile – saliva.

seileach – sallow, salicin(e). **Seileach** is 'a willow', the genus salix. Occasionally found in placenames, as Achnashelloch just north of Lochgilphead, Argyll, but more often in its Scots form *saugh* or *sauch*.

seinn – sound, sonar. **Seinn** means 'sing'.

sgeul – saga. **Sgeul** is 'a story, tale'. The root is found in **soisgeul** 'gospel', the prefix **so-** meaning 'good, favourable', as Scots *sonsie* contrasted with *donsie*. Pitskelly, on the outskirts of Carnoustie, Angus refers historically to a piece of land inhabited by a **sgeulaiche**, a traditional storyteller.

sìor – serein, soirée. **Sìor** means 'long, far off, everlasting'. Serein is heavy late evening dew, and a soirée is an evening entertainment. Serenade is also probably related. The idea is that of late (in the day), extended in time, long drawn out.

slac – slay. **Slac** or **slachd** (and the related **slaic**) means '(to) beat, strike', which was an earlier meaning of 'slay'.

sloc – slough. **Sloc** means 'a pit, a hollow'. An occasional feature of placenames, as Slockavullin, **Sloc a' Mhuilinn** 'the Hollow of the Mill' in Knapdale, Argyll.

stàilinn – Stalinist. **Stàilinn** is 'steel', another cognate.

MISCELLANEOUS

talamh – <u>tell</u>uric. **Talamh** is 'the earth', and the various tell- compounds in English relate to the earth. A common compound is **crith-thalmhainn** 'earthquake'.

teile – tilia. **Teile** means 'lime' (tree and fruit) and Tilia is the botanical term for the lime/linden tree. Lime in English refers to two quite different trees, the Germanic-named linden (*line* in Old English) and the Arabic-named citrus with its round green limes. That both are now called lime is just a coincidence, and since **teile** refers to the linden/lime it shouldn't be used for the citrus tree and its fruits. **Liomaid chruinn** (round lemon) or something similar might be better for the fruit.

tòir – Tory. **Tòir** means 'search, pursuit', and an Irish form of it was used to describe British royalists in Ireland in the 17th century.

uileann – ulna, ell, <u>el</u>bow. **Uileann** means 'elbow', and ulna is a bone of the forearm. An ell was an old measurement of length from the elbow to the fingertips.

Borrowings include:

balbh – <u>balb</u>utient. **Balbh** means 'dumb, mute' and balbutient is a classical cognate meaning stammering, stuttering, a sense which **balbh** also had in earlier Irish. Borrowed from Latin.

balla – bailey. **Balla** is 'a wall'. A bailey was an outer wall in mediaeval castles, and is the origin of the Old Bailey in London. Borrowed from English.

bleideag – blade. **Bleideag** is a '(snow) flake' and blade refers to a <u>small</u> leaf, which explains the diminutive **-ag**. Borrowed from Norse, a good source of words for snow unlike, say, the Western Isles, where it is relatively uncommon.

bolt – bolt. **Bolt** means 'wallpaper' in modern Gaelic, and is borrowed from English bolt, a roll of wallpaper, cloth etc.

GAELIC AND ENGLISH

borb – <u>barb</u>arian, rhu<u>barb</u>. **Borb** means 'fierce'. Borrowed from Latin. The Britons must have heard themselves so described during the Roman occupation. The Roman historian Tacitus, in his *Agricola* (a history of Roman campaigns in Britain during the 1st century A.D.) refers several times to the Britons as barbarians. The word was regularly used to describe anyone or anything that was not Greek or Roman, hence the foreign import rhubarb.

caineal – cane. **Caineal** is 'cinnamon', and the reference is to its hollow, cane-like sticks. Borrowed from Scots, but ultimately from Latin.

cidhis – (dis)<u>guise</u>. **Cidhis** is 'a mask, visor', i.e. something which disguises your appearance. Borrowed from Scots.

cnapach – knave. **Cnapach** is 'a young lad'. Borrowed from Norse.

cochall – cowl. Both words mean 'a hood' such as worn by monks etc. **Cochall** also means husk or shell and is often used with **c(h)ridhe** 'heart' to signify fear, fright. Borrowed from Latin.

coineanach – con(e)y. Borrowed from English.

cop – cap, cope(stone). **Cop** is 'foam, spume'. The idea is the <u>top</u> of the waves. Borrowed from English.

còrd – accord. **Còrd** means '(to) agree with, be agreeable, enjoy'. For the prefix in English compare **rùchd** §6, and **brù** and **liubhair** in this section. Borrowed from English.

crèis – crass, grease. **Crèis** is 'grease, fat'. The general idea is 'fat, thick'. The Gaelic is borrowed from Scots but is ultimately from Latin via French. Crassus was a well-known family name in ancient Rome, borne notably by Marcus Licinius Crassus, a member of the first triumvirate with Pompey and Caesar.

cropaig – crappit. The Gaelic, borrowed from Scots, occurs in the words **ceann-cropaig** 'crappit heid' (stuffed head). The reference is to a cod or haddock head stuffed with oatmeal, suet, onions etc, and cooked. Some Lewis speakers have **ceann propaig**. See also the end of §5.

crùb – creep. **Crùb** means 'crouch, squat'. Borrowed from Norse. See also §1.

currac – kerchief, curch. **Currac** is 'a cap, bonnet, a covering for the head' (which is the literal meaning of kerchief). Borrowed from Scots.

Dimàirt – Mars, martial. **Dimàirt** is 'Tuesday', the day of Mars (Roman god of war), just as Tuesday is named after the Norse god of war. The Roman version also appears, as might be expected, in the Romance family (French *Mardi*, Italian *Martedí* etc) as well as in the Celtic languages (e.g. Welsh *dydd Mawrth*). Related also is the surname Martin. Borrowed from Latin.

dìt – in<u>dict</u>. **Dìt** means 'condemn'. There was an earlier form *dite*, now obsolete. Borrowed from English or Scots.

Dòmhnaich – dominie, dominion. **Di<u>dòmhnaich</u>** is 'Sunday', i.e. the Lord's day. Borrowed from Latin.

gleansach – glance. **Gleansach** means 'shiny, resplendent, dazzling'. In Scots *glance* meant 'shine, gleam', and the adjective *glancy*, from which the Gaelic is borrowed, means 'shiny'.

ifrinn – infernal. **Ifrinn** means 'hell'. Borrowed from Latin.

laghairt – al<u>ligator</u>. **Laghairt** is 'a lizard', itself also cognate. Early Spanish explorers in the Americas thought that alligators had a resemblance to lizards; the al- prefix is the Spanish definite article *el*. Borrowed from Latin.

liubhair – de<u>liver</u>. Ultimately from Latin, but the Gaelic form points to a borrowing from Scots *liver*, now used in the sense of unloading a ship. Other classical cognates like 'liberal, liberate' etc retain the Latin **b**, whereas 'deliver' matches the Gaelic lenited **b** –

see under lenition in the introduction. For the prefix in English compare **rùchd** §6, and **brù**, **còrd** in this section. There is also a form **lìbhrig**.

lòinidh – loin. **Lòinidh** is 'rheumatism'. English loin is borrowed from earlier French *loigne*, itself from Latin *lumbus* 'loin', hence English 'lumbago'.

long – longship. **Long** means 'a ship'. The term longship historically refers to Viking boats (very familiar to Gaels in the Hebrides), but **long** is generally taken as a borrowing from Latin *navis longa*, 'warship', and apparently explains Loch Long in Argyll.

lòsan – lozenge. **Lòsan** is 'a window pane', originally a diamond-shaped pane within a latticed framework. Lozenge is a rhombus, a diamond-shaped figure. Borrowed from Scots, but of French origin.

màileid – mail. **Màileid** is 'a bag'. Mail was originally a bag for carrying letters etc, but now restricted to the letters themselves. Borrowed from English, which borrowed it from early French.

màl – mail. **Màl** is 'rent' (payment), also the meaning of Scots *mail*, and English 'black<u>mail</u>'. Borrowed from English.

mallachd – malediction. **Mallachd** is 'a curse'. Borrowed from Latin. See also **meall** above in this section.

meirghe – mark, margin. **Meirghe** is 'a banner', with 'mark' in its sense of sign, symbol. Mark earlier had also the meaning 'boundary' – now 'march' – with which margin is a classical cognate. Borrowed from Norse.

modh – mode, modus vivendi. **Modh** means 'manner, manners'. Borrowed from Latin.

muinichill – manacle. **Muinichill** is 'a sleeve'. The idea is something your hand goes through. Related 'hand' words in

Miscellaneous

English are 'manage, manual, manufacture, manipulate' etc. Borrowed from Latin.

mùth – mutate. **Mùth** means '(to) change'. Also cognate are 'moult' and 'mews' (from French), the latter now a fashionable town house, but in origin a building where moulting hawks were kept. Borrowed from Latin, the long **u** of which explains the Gaelic accent.

nòin – noon. The English word now has a **u** sound (see §37), but it was earlier *non*, 'ninth' (hour, referring to a church service time, later shifted back three hours). From the same root is **neòinean** 'daisy', so named because the flower opens out during daylight.[36] Daisy (i.e. day's eye) is similarly named since it resembles the sun with its rays and opens fully only during bright daylight. Borrowed from Latin. Again, the Gaelic accent reflects a long vowel in the Latin.

pasgan – fasces, fascicule, Fascism. **Pasgan** means 'a bundle' and the English words all derive from the Latin *fasces*, 'a bundle of rods', a symbol of authority in Ancient Rome.

peasair – pease. **Peasair** is 'pea'. The Gaelic **s** is usually explained by the fact that pease was singular but was later taken as a plural, and a new singular form pea was created. Borrowed from English or Scots, ultimately from Latin.

piseag – puss. **Piseag** is 'a kitten'. Borrowed from English.

prìomh – prime. Both words borrowed from Latin.

rannsaich – ransack. **Rannsaich** means '(to) investigate, research'. Borrowed from Norse.

---

[36] **Nòin** had a wider sense, including 'afternoon', in earlier Gaelic.

ridire – rider. **Ridire** is 'a knight', and is used, as in English, as the title 'sir'. **Rubha an Ridire** is a promontory at the southern tip of Morvern. Borrowed from English.

sabhal – stable. **Sabhal** is 'a barn'. Borrowed from Latin. The word is quite common in placenames, the best known being Tomintoul, **Tom an t-Sabhail** 'The Hillock of the Barn'.

seòmar – chamber. **Seòmar** is 'a room', borrowed from Scots *chaumer* showing the influence of Norman-French pronunciation (*chambre*).

sglèat – slate. Borrowed from English or Scots, whose earlier form was *sclat*, *skleat* etc.

siùd – shudder. **Siùd** means '(to) swing'. The pronunciation suggests a borrowing from Scots *schewd* (various spellings). **Siùdan** is 'a swing, pendulum'.

spèil – bonspiel. **Spèil** means '(to) skate', and bonspeil is a curling match played on ice. Borrowed from Scots. The Germanic root 'spiel' means 'play', as it did in Scots.

speur – sphere. **Speur** is 'the sky', and a sphere is 'a ball, globe'. Borrowed from Latin. An obscure classical cognate is 'sphairistike', an early name for tennis.

suaip – swap. **Suaip** is 'a likeness, facial resemblance'. This meaning of Scots *swap* (from which **suaip** is apparently borrowed) is quite recent (19th century) and is found mainly in areas where Gaelic has not been spoken for some time, or at all. But the word's origins are Scandinavian, which may have influenced the Gaelic.

tàileasg – table, tablet. **Tàileasg** is 'chess'. The idea is that of a board (compare **bòrd** - table) game. For the absence of **b** see **neul** above in this section. A wonderful collection of mediaeval chessmen (**fir-tàilisg**), most of them carved from walrus tusks, was discovered in sand dunes at Uig, Lewis in 1831. Borrowed from English.

Miscellaneous

toinn – twine. **Toinn** means '(to) twist'. Borrowed from Norse.

trèanaig – train (get fit). This word, chosen at random, illustrates the fact that when Gaelic borrows a verb from English, it generally uses the present participle (-ing) form but drops the **n**. There are dozens of such borrowings in modern Gaelic.

trusgan – truss, trousseau. **Trusgan** is 'clothing'. Borrowed from English.

uimhir – numeral. **Uimhir** means 'a quantity, number'. The initial **n** has dropped off in Gaelic due to confusion over the definite article, *an nuimhir* becoming **an uimhir**. Borrowed from Latin. For a similar confusion compare **deanntag** 'nettle', where the **d** (like **t**, see §29) was originally part of the article.[37] Also found are the forms **feanntag** (see §10), **eanntag** and **neanntag,** but the last two are no longer recommended forms, even though the original Gaelic form began with **n**, and appears in Invernenty 'a confluence where nettles thrive' (Glen and River), a couple of miles west of Loch Doine in Balquhidder, and Loch (with Glen and River) Nant south of Taynuilt in Argyll.

ung – unguent, anoint. **Ung** means 'anoint'. Borrowed from Latin.

---

[37] The opposite occurs in **ràc** 'drake', where the **d** has mistakenly been regarded as part of the article, which it obviously isn't since the word is borrowed from English 'drake'. The more logical form **dràc** is also found.

INDEX

This list contains all the Gaelic words discussed above. They are given in alphabetical order along with the section(s) in which they can be found, for easy reference. I haven't attempted to give any pronunciation guides for the Gaelic words; interested readers may find *A Gaelic Alphabet – a guide to the pronunciation of Gaelic letters and words* (New Argyll Publishing 2018), mentioned in the introduction, helpful.

abstol §1	allt §42	at §20
abharsaic §16	alt §20, §31	athair §20
acair §19	altram §42	bàbhan §31
achd §6	amadan §7	bac §19
adag §13, §16	a-màireach §31	bachall §42
aghann §42	amar §31	bad §8
aifreann §31	amh §31	bagaid §13
aigeann §13	amhach §31	baile §17
aileag §16	a-mhàin §31	baist §20, §40
aingeal §40	àmhainn §31	balbh §42
ainm §41	anam §33	balg §12, §42
ainneamh §19	a-nochd §6	balla §42
ainnir §19	aodann §7, §32	balt §1
airgead §7	aoine §32	banaltram §42
àirneis §16	aois §30	bann §19
àird §7	aon §32	barantas §1
aire §20	arbhar §42	bàs §19
aisean §31	arm §41	bathar §1
aisling §39	àros §22	beach §33
aiteann §42	às §22	bean §30
aitheamh §20	asgaill §40	beannachd §6, §19, §34

INDEX

beatha §33
beirm §19
beir §35
beithe §35
beò §30
beurla §40
bile(ag) §19
binn §42
biodag §7
blàth §19
bleadraich §7
bleideag §42
bleoghain(n) §40
bloigh §13
bò §30 §39
boc §37
bòc §37
bòcan §37
bodhar §7
bolt §42
bonaid §7
bonn §19
borb §42
bothar §1
brà §30
bragh §13
bràthair §19
breith §40
brìgh §42
briogais §13

briosgaid §13
bris(t) §40
brisgean §13
brod §42
brot §28
brù §42
bruadar §39
brùid §7
brùth §42
buachaille §39
buaic §1
buaidh §39
buideal §7
buidhe §42
buidhinn §1
burmaid §1
cabar §1
cabstair §1
caibeal §1, §4
caibideil §1, §4
cailc §4, §17
cailis §4
cailleach §5, §17
càin §5
cainb §2, §41
caineal §42
Caingis §5
cairt §31
cairteal §3
càise §4

Càisg §5, §13
càl §31
calc §17
call 'lose' §2, §18
call 'hazel' §18
Callainn §17
calltainn §2
calman §41
cam §2
can §2, §4
caoch §32
caog §13
caoin §2, §32
caol §32
caomh §2, §32
caor §20
caora §20
car §42
caraid §4, §7
carbad §1
carrasan §42
cartan §5
cas 'steep' §2, §22
cas 'leg' §22, §31
casad §7
cast §2, §31
castan §4
cathair §4
ceall §2
ceangal §13

ceann §5, §33
ceart §34
ceil §2, §35
ceilp §17
cèir §35
ceist §3
ceò §23
ceud §2, §7
ciar §23
cidhe §3
cidhis §42
cill §36
cìobair §1
ciobhal §42
cìs §19, §36
ciste §4
cistin §40
ciudha §3
ciùin §30
clag §13
clann §5, §19
claon §2, §32
clàr §42
clèireach §35
clìceach §36
cliù §2
clò §30
clobha §30
clòimh §5, §37
cluas §2, §22

clùd §7
cnap §31
cnapach §42
cnò §2, §37
cnuas §39
cò §2
cochall §42
cogall §13
còig §5
coilear §17
coille §2, §18
coineanach §42
coinneal §19
coire §42
còisir §40
coisrig §40
colbh §41
comann – see introduction
connlach §42
conntraigh §13
cop §42
còrcair §5, §37
corc §40
còrd §42
còrn §2
còs §30
craiceann §23
cràin §19
creamh §2

creid §35
crèis §42
creubh §2
criathar §2
cridhe §2, §7, §36
crò §2
cròc §4
croch §37
crodh §2
crog §13
crog(an) §13
crois §22
cropaig §42
cruach §2
cruaidh §2, §39
crùb §42
crùbach §1
cruinn §38
cù §2
cuach §3
cuag §2, §13
Cuaigear §3
cuan §2, §20
cuango §3
cuaraidh §3
cuarantain §3
cùbaid §1, §5, §7
cùbair §1
cuid §3, §5, §38
cuidhteas §3

INDEX

cuilc §42
cuileag §42
cuilean §23
cuileann §2, §38
cuimhne §38
cuin §2
cuing §38
cuinnse §3
cùis §38
cuithe §5
cùl §38
culaidh §2
cullach §42
cuman §42
cumhang §42
cùmhnant §38
cuota §3
curach §38
curaidh §4
currac §42
dà §7
dail §17
dàil §42
dàimh §42
dall §42
damh §7, §31
dàn §31
darach §7
deachd §6
deagh §34

deamhais §31
deanntag §42
dearbh §40
dearg §13
deas §22, §34
deich §7, §35
dèilig §17
deimhinne §35
deisciobal §35
deud §7
deug §13
deur §7
dia §30
diathad §7
dìblidh §36
dlleachdan §19
Dimàirt §42
dimeas §19
dìreach §34
dìt §42
(an)-diugh §42
do 'to' §7
do 'your' §7
dòcha §37
dogha §13
doire §7
Dòmhnaich §42
donn §37
donnal §42
doras §7

drannd §31
draoch §7
draoidh §32
drògaid §37
droigheann §7
drùchd §20
druid §7
dual §7
duais §38
duille(ag) §7
dùn §7
dùsal §38
Eabhra §16
each §3, §34
eadar §7, §33
eaglais §13
ealtainn §23
Eanraig §16
eàrr §42
eas §20
easag §10
easbaig §40
easbaloid §40
easgann §13
eidheann §20
eige §10
eigh §42
eighe §13
(an) Eilbheis §16
èildear §17

175

eile §42
eileatrom §10
eilid §35
èirich §42
èirig §35
eisimpleir §35
eisir §27
èiteag §16
eug §19
eun §20
facal §9, §31
fadhail §9
fàidh §7, §9
failc §10
failm §10
fàilte §9
fàinne §10
fàir §9
fàisg §9
fàl §9
falc §10
fallainn(g) §5
falt §9, §31
fànas §9
fann §9
faodhail §32
faoileag §32
fàs 'grow' §10, §22
fàs 'empty' §9, §22
fàsach §9

fasgadh §13
fastadh §9
feachd §9, §33
feall §33
feallsanach §33
fear §9, §33
feàrn (Intr.)
fearsaid §9
feart §9, §33
feasgar §9, §20, §34
fèileadh §9
feith §9
fèith §9
feun §9, §15
fhuair §42
fianais §9
fighe §10
fill §9
fine §9
fiodh §9
fion §9
fionn §19
fìor §9, §36
fios §8, §9
flath §9
fleistear §10
fleòdradh §7
fliuch §10
foghar §14 (Intr.)
foill §9

foinne §10
fòirneart §34
follaiseach §11
fonn 'tune' §11, §19
fonn 'land' §19
fraoch §10, §32
fras §10
freumh §10
fusgan §13
gad §12
gàir (Intr.)
gairm (Intr.)
galan §17
galar §13
gamhainn §14 (Intr.)
garbh §14
garg §31
gàrradh §12
gart §14
gas §14, §22
gead §34
geal §12, §34
geall §18
geamhradh §14
gean §13
geanm-chnò §4
gearan §13
geimheal §36
geòla §12
gheat §12

INDEX

giall §42
gilb §23
gille §13, §18
gin §13, §36
gionach §13, §36
glag §13
glaodh §13, §32
glas 'lock' §13, §20
glas 'grey, green' §42
gleansach §42
gleus §19
glùn §13
gnàth(s) §13, §31
gnè §13
gnog §13
go(i)rt §12
gobhal §42
goile §37
goirtean §14
goistidh §40
gràdh §7
gràinne §13
greadan §8, §33
greas §42
greideal §7, §13
greigh §35
greim §13
grothlach §30
grùdaire §7
grùid §7

gruth §13
gual §13
gun §13
hama §16
hocaidh §16
iall §20
iarmailt §10
iasg §13, §20
ifrinn §42
imcheist §3
imleag §13, §16
imlich §42
Inid §7
innis §42
ìobair §42
ionga §40
iongnadh §13
ionnsaich §42
ite §20
iuchair §5
labhair §42
ladarna §7
lag §13, §19
laghairt §42
làmh §20, §40
làn §20
langasaid §31
lann §19
laoch §32
làr §20, §31

leabhar §33
leac §20, §34
leagh §13
leamhan §40
learag §13
leathann §20
leig §19
lèine §42
leistear §10
leòr §30
leth §42
leugh §13
lì §30
liagh §42
liath §20 (twice)
lighiche §36
lìnig (Intr.)
lìomh §42
lìon 'fill' §36
lìon 'flax' §42
lios §20
lite §20
litir §36
liubhair §42
liuthad §20
lobh §42
lòchran §37
lòinidh §42
long §42
lòsan §42

Gaelic and English

loth 'marsh' §37
loth 'colt' §20
luach §39
luachair §39
luaidh §42
luan §39
luath §20
lùb §1
luchraban §42 (lugha)
lùdag §7
lugha §42
luidhear §30
Lunnainn §19
lurach §39
luspardan §42 (lugha)
MacMhànais §15
madainn §7
mag §13, §31
màg §19
maide §8
màileid §42
mair §31
màl §42
mallachd §42
màm §42
manach §31
manadh §31
mannas §19
manntach §19
maoin §32

maor §32
maorach §32
maoth §32
marbh §31
marc §42
margadh §13
matamataig §28
màthair §31
meadhan §33, §34
mealbhag §42
meall §42
mean §33
meanmna §33, §34
mearachd §42
meas 'respect' §19
meas 'fruit' §42
measg §33
measg(aich) §13
meath §32
meidh §35
meil §42
meirg §13
meirghe §42
meud §7
mial §23
miann §36
mias §19
mil §36
minig §12
mìog §23

mìos §19, §36
miosa §42
miotas §28
mire §36
mislean §40
mòd §7
modh §42
molach §42
moll §18
monadh §42
monais §42
mòr §42
mosach §8
muc §23
mùch §23
muileann §38
muineal §38
muinichill §42
muir §38
mult §42
mùr §42
mùth §42
nàmhaid §42
naodh §32
nead §8, §33, §34
nèamh §34
neart §34
neul §42
nigh §13
nighean §13

178

INDEX

nochd 'night' §7
nochd 'naked' §42
nòin §42
Nollaig §17
nuadh §30 §39
òb §1, §16
obair §1
obann §19 (bonn)
ochd §6
òg §19, §37
oighre §16
oir §42
oitir §36
òl §20
(an) Òlaind §16
olann §42
olc §37
òmar §16
onair §16
onfhadh §7
òr §37
òraid §7
os §22
osan §16
òsta §16
othaisg §30
othar §20
òtrach §20, §37
paidirean §7
pàillean §30

pailm §17
pàiste §40
partan §5
pasgan §42
peacadh §34
peasair §42
pèileag §13
peileir §17
peirceall §42
pìob §1
piobar §1
pioghaid §7
piseag §42
piuthar §21
plangaid §1
plaosg §32
pleadh §23
ploc §1
pòg §13
pònair §1
pòr §23
pòs §19, §23
praighig §5
prais §1
preas §20
prìomh §42
pucaid §1
pùdar §5
putan §1
rag §13

raineach §10
ràmh §42
rannsaich §42
rathad §31
reachd §6, §33, §34
rèilig §35
riaghailt §36
riamh §20
riasg §42
ridire §42
rìgh §36
ro §20
rong §37
ronn §37
ros §20, §22
roth §42
ruadh §10, §39
rùchd §6
rùda §40
rug §13
rùn §42
sàbaid §7
sabhal §42
sagart §13
saidhe §25
saighead §7
sail §42
saill §18
sainnseal §19, §25
sàl §24

salach §42
salm §20
samhail §42
samhradh §42
saoghal §13, §32
saoil §32
saor §20
saothair §32
sàth §42
sè §24
seabhag §25
seac §33
seach §34
seach(ad) §3
seachd §20, §24, §34
sealg §20
seamrag §13
sean §34
seanchaidh §41
searbh §42
seàrr §24
seas §22, §33
seasg 'dry' §13, §33
seiceal §25
seiche §35
sèid §8, §24
seile §42
seileach §42
seinn §42
seòmar §42

seun §15
sgadan §26
sgàil §26
sgainneal §13, §19
sgàird §13
sgait §13
sgalag §26
sgàld §13
sgar §26
sgàrlaid §7, §13
sgath §13
sgàth §26, §31
sgeallag §13
sgeap §13
sgeilb §23
sgeilp §26, §35
sgeir §13, §35
sgeul §42
sgiamhach §26
sgil 'skill' §13
sgil 'to shell' §26
sgillinn §26
sgioba §1, §26
sgiobair §13
sgiort(a) §13
sgìre §26
sgiùrs §13
sglèat §42
sgoil §13, §17
sgoilt §13

sgòr §13
sgòth §26
sgraing §26
sgread §7
sgreuch §13, §26
sgrìobh §13
sgriubha §13
sgròb §13
sgrùd §7, §13
sguab §38
sgudal §23
sgùm §13
sia §24
siabann §1
sine §20
sinnsear §36
sìoda §7
sionn §20
sìor §42
sir §20
sìth §36
siùd §42
siùrsach §25
slac §42
slaic §23
slàn §40
slaod §32
slat §23
sleuchd §21
sliabh §1

INDEX

slìogach §13
slis §20
sloc §42
smachd §7, §23
smal §23
smalan §23
smàrag §23
smodal §37
smug §13, §23
snaidh §7
snaidhm §23
snàig §13
snàmh §23
snaoisean §32
snàth §31
snàthad §23
sneachd §23, §30
sneadh §23, §24, §33
snèap §23
snighe §30
snìomh §23
soc §24
sònraichte §37
sòrn §21, §37
spaideil §7
spàl §31
spann §23
speach §23
spealt §33
spèil §42
speur §42
spìocach §19, §23.
spiorad §7
spong §21, §37
spor §37
sporan §23, §37, §40
spreadh §13
sprèidh §23, §35
spùill §38
sràbh §27
srac §23
srad §27
sràid §7
srath §27
sream §27
sreang §27, §33
sreath §40
srian §21
sringlean §27
sroghall §21
srùb §27
sruth §23, §27
stad §7
staid §7
stail §33
stàilinn §42
stang §13, §40
stanna §23
staoin §32
steall §33
steàrnan §23
steatasgop §28
stràc §31
suain §20, §24
suaineadh §21
suaip §42
sùbailte §1
sùgh §13
suidhe §7
sùil §38
sùist §21
sùlaire §38
susbaint §40
tabh §29
tadhal §29
taigeis §29
taigh see teach
tàileasg §42
tàillear §17
taing §28
tàirneanach §40
tàladh §31
talamh §42
talan §29
talla §29
tàmh §23
tana §28
taois §23
taoitear §32
tarbh §23

Gaelic and English

tàrr §28
tart §28
tàth §23
teach §23, §28, §34
teanga §33
teann §19
tèarmann §34
teile §42
teirm §35
teisteanas §35
teth §20
tha §23
thig §23
thu §28
tiachd §6
tiota §29
tìr §36
tiugh §13, §28
tlàth §28
tobar §19
todha §29
togsaid §29
toil §28
toinn §42
tòir §42
tolm §29
tom §37
tomhas §19
tonnag §37
torrannach §28

tràigh §13
tràill §17
trang §31
tre §28
treabh §28
trèanaig §42
treas §33
trì §28
trianaid §7
tròcair §39
trod §28
trombaid §37
trosg §40
truagh §39
truaill §28, §39
trusgan §42
tu §28
tuam §39
tuarastal §31
tuath §38
tughadh §28
tùis §28
tulach §28
tùs §38
uabhar §39
uachdar §20
uair §16
uan §15
uasal §20
ubh §38

ubhal §1
uchd §6, §20
uèir §1
ugan §10
ugh §38
ùghdar §7
uidh §7, §20, §38
ùig §13
uile §20
uileann §42
uimhir §42
uinneag §19
uinnean §38
uircean §20, §38
uisge §8, §13
ulag §20
ulbhach §20
umha(i)l §16
umpaidh §29
ung §42
(an) Ungair §16
ùr §20
vals §1
watt §1

www.ingramcontent.com/pod-product-compliance
Lightning Source LLC
Chambersburg PA
CBHW071345080526
44587CB00017B/2976